Choices:

Escaping the Illusion of Being a Victim

by

Nancy Fischer

Requests for such permission should be addressed to:

WriteOn Publishing Co., L.L.C.
P. O. Box 308
Yellow Springs, Ohio 45387

Fischer, Nancy
    Choices: Escaping the Illusion of Being a Victim

The goddess graphic on the cover and throughout the text was designed by Contemporary Fine Artist, Eve Margo Withrow, www.evemargowithrow.com, and was used with permission.

Cover Design: Manjari Graphics
Cover Art: Eve Margo Withrow
Cover Photo: Michael Ayers
Layout: J. L. Saloff
Fonts used: Goudy, Papyrus

10-Digit ISBN: 0-9774183-0-8
13-Digit ISBN: 978-0-9774183-0-5
Library of Congress Control Number: 2005910376
Copyright information available upon request.

First Edition:

Printed on acid free paper in The United States of America

Dedication:

To Dan,
the mirror reflecting that I am
worthy to be loved.

and

To Joerdie,
who loves me enough to hold my feet to the fire
even at the risk of getting burned.

Table of Contents

Section One: It's Only a Game

Section Two: Life Before Memories

Section Three: I Find Love, But Not Necessarily Happiness

Section Four: AHA!

Section Five: Alternative Therapies

Section Six: Out of My Comfort Zone and Into the Light

Acknowledgments

While our spiritual journeys may be solo adventures, writing a book is not. I could not have completed this cathartic work without the many beloved souls who agreed to participate in my dramas on classroom earth. To the friends and loved ones I have mentioned, and the many more I have not, my heartfelt thanks:

God/Goddess and my heavenly guides and teachers

Tom Bird—Writing coach and mentor who knows how to bridge the gap between idea and paper

Jamie Saloff—Manuscript formatting and layout and "go to" person for all things publishing

Manjari Henderson—Cover construction and design

Eve Margo Withrow—Cover artist who shares a path from victimhood to gratitude

Elizabeth Byrd and Curt Branum—Diagonal Designs, website design

George Weinstein—Copy editor

Michael Ayers—Cover photographer

My family, both those related by blood and those who share a deep soul connection, Dan and Erica Fischer, Joerdie, Eric, Ian, Katie, Kaya, Scott, Megan and Wyatt Fisher, Jim Bowsher, Aria Magi, Rachel Moulton, Janet, Steve, Andrew and Elliot Schuler, my sister, Peggy Matheny and my parents, Leo Peterson and Mary Peterson Hall. I love you all.

And finally, just a few of the many friends and teachers who have offered special encouragement and wise counsel, Marty Cheney, Linda Cyran, Marie Fairchild, Susan Fantz, Billie Friend, Helen George, Jahwara Giddings, Marjorie Flinn Gratz, Peggy Hanna, Lee Hardacre, Kathie Hassenauer, Joyce Hutto and her beloved Bill, Shirley Jacquay, Annie Kennedy, Sally Kennedy, Dave Martino, John McMullin, Jodie Simmons, the Six Figure Posse, David Sohn, Dave Ullery, Skip Wallach, Peggy Welty, Charlie and Emma Zaenglein, and Frazier and Lucy and my other animal friends and companions.

Section One:
It's Only a Game

1
Classroom Earth

Welcome to Classroom Earth where souls from all over the Universe come to experience all the human form has to offer.

In order to evolve to a higher state of enlightenment, each soul must encounter every human condition and emotion through a series of lifetimes—or earthwalks—to learn the lessons these experiences offer, according to Michael Newton, Ph.D., in his case studies of life between lives that he chronicles in his books *Journey of Souls, Destiny of Souls,* and *Life Between Lives.*

To accomplish these goals, souls rely on help from other like souls called soul groups because they travel together lifetime after lifetime learning and growing together. I envision a soul group as a sort of improvisational troupe that meets before each lifetime and agrees what role each will play in the drama that is about to unfold. Carolyn Myss refers to these agreements in her best-selling book, *Sacred Contracts.*

If a soul wants to learn the lesson of empowerment, it might choose a lifetime as a single mother with an abusive boyfriend. One of the other souls in its group would agree to assume the role of the boyfriend and others, the roles of her children, parents, and friends. They would incarnate on earth in the human situations they agreed upon, and play out the roles of the drama. In the next lifetime, the soul group might choose the same lessons, but each soul would assume a different part in the drama in which they are participating. Perhaps the next time the abusive boyfriend will play the role of the single mother he has abused in the previous life so that ultimately each soul can experience each role.

Like any improv group, the soul group has only a bit of a story line, but once it has been established, the Universe will step in and provide the specific scenarios for the group to follow. From there it becomes like a game whose objective is for the souls to wake up and remember that only love is real. Everything else is just an illusion of fear in one form or another.

To make the game more interesting, the soul's memory of the agreement is wiped clean before it enters the human experience. The human child will be born into the family and circumstances it agreed to beforehand, but it will not remember. While the soul, now in human form, has a basic outline to follow by virtue of where and when it enters the game, the Universe will create the specific scenarios along the way to provide the players the opportunity to learn the lessons they agreed upon in their sacred contracts. The souls participating in the game of life have choices of how to respond to each situation. They can respond with love or fear. Their choice will determine the outcome of each drama. If a soul does not learn the lesson on the first try, which it rarely does, the Universe will provide new opportunities to learn. That is why some humans appear to make the same "mistakes" over and over. It is why a woman, for example, would go from abusive relationship to abusive relationship. The lesson she came to learn was self-love, and the means she chose to learn it was abuse. It would appear that she continues to make the same mistake over and over again, when in fact, there are no mistakes. Everything happens for a reason, and everything happens with the express agreement of the souls involved by virtue of their sacred contracts.

But what if the sacred contract involves something humans would consider heinous like sexual abuse or murder? Is it still sacred? Yes, because in the spirit realm there is no judgment attached to any of these experiences since they are all agreed upon in advance, and they are all illusions we have created for the lessons we came to learn. Judgment is a human characteristic. It does not exist in the spirit realm. That is precisely why spirits need the human form to learn these experiences. The reality of the illusion is that there are no victims, only volunteers. There are no winners or losers, only participants in the illusions of our own creating. Life is not a competition, but an opportunity to learn and grow and move ever closer to our own divinity.

One of the beauties of the Universe is that we are all one, all part of the same God source. There is no race, no gender, no class distinction, no separation of any kind. Those again are human phenomenon and ones we choose with each earthwalk. Souls ascend to higher levels of enlightenment, but rather than being ego-based where one soul is considered superior as it would be on earth, more highly evolved souls help teach other souls to bring them along. It is like the Africana philosophy of "lift as you climb" where as people attain some human measure of success, they will simultaneously work to help others advance. There are none of the illusions of separation in the spirit realm that humans have created to delineate one group from another. We are all one with one Creator and one common goal. In the spirit realm there is no right or wrong because everything is done from love.

The same could be true on earth were it not for the human ego. The only judgments are those created by humans. They are not imposed by God/Goddess, because the Creator is pure light and love. It is impossible to do anything without the knowledge and acceptance of God/Goddess who created everything.

Frequently when I talk with people about sacred contracts and Classroom Earth, they will look shocked. Obviously concerned for my eternal soul, they will ask if I am a Christian. I am not certain how to answer. I am definitely a follower of the teachings and philosophy of Jesus, which are love, peace, and harmony, but that is also true of the Buddha and many other of the ascended masters who taught a similar philosophy. Assigning a label does not fit. I find that the doctrines of any organized religion are too limiting and are based on fear. I would agree with Mae Ward when she said of organized religion, "Your God is too small." There is nothing wrong with organized religion, of course, because like everything else on Classroom Earth, each of the participants, the religious leaders as well as the followers, chose these roles before they began their current earthwalk. Like the rest of us, they are just playing the roles in the dramas the Universe creates.

The notion that there is a separate God/Goddess for the Christians, the Jews, the Muslims, the Buddhists, the Hindus and all the other religions of the world and that only by following their own prescribed doctrines can one hope to reach heaven is absurd. As Mahatma Gandhi said, "God has no religion." There is only one God/Goddess, who loves us all equally because we are all one. The idea of separation is an illusion created by the Universe and fed by the human ego like all the other dramas in our human lives so that we will discover our own divinity.

In our human dramas on Classroom Earth, the spirits incarnated in human form feel all the emotions and pain that accompany the human experience. That is the point. Even though we have agreed to the experiences through our sacred contracts, because our memories are blocked when we enter the human bodies, we experience the trauma of abuse or the frustration of being a victim. It is not until we begin to wake up and remember our agreements that we can comprehend the illusion and decide to end it. We can change the game by changing the rules. If a spirit has chosen the human role of victim, it will continue to find itself in situations where it is a victim. The Universe will continue to provide opportunities, frequently escalating in severity by human standards, until the spirit "wakes up" and refuses to play the role anymore. If the lesson is self-love, for example, the means to learning that lesson will be something that creates the illusion of low self-esteem such as abuse.

The Universe will continue to provide the dramas of abuse until the participant either learns the lesson or decides to leave this earthwalk and try again later. There is no disgrace in returning to try the lesson a second or even a third time. Disgrace is a human illusion.

While we may continue to experience the human dramas, it is how we respond to them that matters in escaping from the illusion of being a victim. We can either continue to have situations happen to us or we can begin to take responsibility for our actions and our lives and thank the Universe for what it has done for us in order that we might learn the lessons we came to learn. It is a choice.

The lessons I came to learn are self-love and empowerment. The means I chose to learn them were sexual abuse from my father and non-nurturing and emotional abuse from my mother. I was apparently a recalcitrant student because it took nearly a half-century for me to begin to wake up and learn the lessons. Even then it took something as dramatic as flashbacks to finally get my attention.

Along the way the Universe provided a myriad of opportunities for my education.

Section Two:
Life Before
Memories

2
We Put the *Fun* in Dysfunctional

I spent my childhood in an upper lower-class neighborhood in the old house on Harrison Street in Wapakoneta, Ohio, that my father purchased while my mother was in the hospital giving birth to my older sister Peggy. Mother always hated the house, with its damp, musty basement and no formal living or dining rooms in which to entertain friends. To say the house was a fixer-upper was an understatement, but fix it up they did. For the thirty-three years my parents lived there, it seemed they were always in the midst of some new remodeling project.

Mother chose an alcoholic, misogynistic German father and an uneducated, fearful mother to experience non-nurturing in this earthwalk. My mother would never discuss her childhood with me. I later came to realize that like me, she simply could not remember. Her behavior was typical of a woman who had chosen extreme emotional and probably sexual abuse as a human experience. Even as an adult, she behaved as a frightened, wounded child, because in her human experience, she was. At times she also showed fierce independence and disregard for rules that frequently landed her in trouble. The result, however, allowed her to play the victim role with great flair. Her sister Helen provided some insight into my mother:

> "Papa always said girls shouldn't ride bicycles,
> so I never learned how. Mary, of course, just went

ahead and did it. I never learned to swim either, but she did. She did whatever she wanted. I just did what I was told.

Papa said girls didn't need to go to school because they were just going to get married anyway. Aunt Emma talked to him, and then we were allowed to go, but all through school your mother and I only had two dresses each, which we alternated wearing. We got to attend high school but there was never any question that we wouldn't be going on to college. The first chance your mother got to get away she jumped on."

Grandma Speidel was less strict than Grandpa, but she was extremely negative and fearful in the role she played. She responded to almost any idea with "You daresn't do that." Growing up in that household did little to build my mother's self-esteem, which was obviously the lesson she agreed to learn. She was still in high school when she claimed to be pregnant and married the boyfriend with whom she had been sexually active. It is unclear whether Mother actually believed she was pregnant or was just trying to escape an unpleasant home life, but not unexpectedly, the marriage lasted only a few years and produced no children.

She told me in the years shortly before her passing that it was during her brief marriage that she met and fell in love with a young man, the cousin of her husband, who was not only married but had young children. The man wanted to divorce his wife and marry her, but not wanting to break up his family, my mother refused. Instead, she began a relationship with the man that lasted nearly fifty years, until his death.

Marked by the human stigma and humiliation of a teenage marriage and subsequent divorce, and in love with a man she could never have, my mother's human prospects must have seemed grim. However, to get to experience being a victim, they were phenomenal.

It is not surprising that when she met my father, who chose the role of a rather handsome and charming, if not overly ambitious, young rogue, she quickly married him. She was just twenty-two. It was 1943, and from the human standpoint, my mother probably felt that he was the best she could hope for under the circumstances. In reality, of course, he was the perfect teacher for the lessons she agreed to tackle.

Whatever her human dreams had been, it was apparent that my mother was unhappy with her lot in life. She was always angry and frustrated, and as our contract dictated, it was usually with me. Our contract began immediately. Almost from birth our relationship was hostile. It was not the type of conflict that most mothers and daughters go through during puberty. This was an obvious, deep-seated resentment we shared. Mother agreed to have an explosive temper and be prone to tantrums. I responded by becoming incorrigible, almost openly hostile toward her.

My older sister Peggy chose a decidedly different human experience to learn many of the same lessons I chose. She became totally passive. While I went out of my way to do the opposite of what my mother wanted, Peggy would acquiesce without question. In essence Peggy and I chose the same dynamic as Mother and her sister Helen for our earthwalks together.

It is difficult for me to be objective about my father from a human standpoint because our sacred contract was so much different from that with my mother. I always preferred him because he was approachable, and I always felt that he loved me. Part of my contract with him, however, included him manipulating me and my relationships with other people so that it was often my dad and me against the world. This was especially true of my relationship with my mother where he would play us against each other. It was an interesting aspect of our contracts together because it always kept the wedge between my mother and me, and thus made her behavior even less nurturing and mine more incorrigible.

When Mother passed over, I went through boxes of family photos from all stages of our lives. My father was an amateur photographer. While there were probably hundreds of pictures of Peggy as an infant and toddler with loving descriptions handwritten on the back by my mother, I found only two pictures of me as a baby. In the first I was less than a year old and Mother was attempting to hold me as I struggled to push her away. The other was the only family portrait I found of the four of us. It was not actually a family picture at all, but rather a bizarre and revealing glimpse into the family dynamic we chose. Instead of the four of us together in one picture, it was two 8"x10" photos placed in a hinged frame to make it appear as one. One picture was of Mother, her arm lovingly around Peggy, both of them smiling. The other was me with my father, and we too appeared happy to be together.

By human standards our family was certainly crazy and dysfunctional, but from the spiritual standpoint, we all played our parts in the dramas we created exactly as we agreed. I don't believe any of us could have chosen more powerful teachers for the lessons we came to learn.

3
Not All
Angels Have Wings

Looking back at my childhood, I am somewhat amazed by the intensity of the lessons I chose to tackle although I understand we never agree to more than we are ready to handle. To make the journey a little easier, the Universe always stepped in and provided angels in the form of caring adults outside my chosen family.

Charlie and Emma Zaenglein were two such people. They spent the winters in Florida, but each spring I eagerly awaited their return to their house on River Street.

Charlie was a retired school teacher, tall, rail thin with a shock of thick white hair peeking out from under his ever-present painting cap. He was probably seventy, but to my young eyes I was certain he was at least one hundred. The Zaengleins owned several rental houses in the neighborhood, which Charlie constantly maintained, thus accounting for the painting cap. They also owned the building that housed Maxson's Grocery, a Mom and Pop store that sold penny candy to the neighborhood children. Charlie and Emma's house was in the back of the grocery. I spent many hours visiting with them, hearing of their travels and sipping Kool-Aid from tall aluminum glasses. Most of the time I followed Charlie around as he tended his yard and gardens. The backyard was a paradise with fruit trees, a grape vineyard, and rows and rows of flower and vegetable gardens. The Auglaize River bordered the entire south side of the property, and although we never kept any of the fish we caught, Charlie showed me how to bait a hook and fish along the banks of the river.

As I tagged along behind him, Charlie would teach me a new word every day, telling me the meaning and how to spell it. The next day he would quiz me on the word, and if I could remember the spelling and meaning, we would move on to a new word. It was no wonder I was an avid reader by the time I reached kindergarten.

While I'm sure that the Zaengleins never suspected the sexual abuse, they couldn't miss the screaming coming from our house. My contract with my mother was much less subtle than the one with my father. If we were home, the odds were high that we would be fighting. The whole neighborhood could hear us. From the human perspective the Zaengleins recognized a bright little girl in need of nurturing, which they willingly provided. They treated me with respect and opened my eyes to a world outside my immediate neighborhood by telling me stories about their travels. What Charlie and Emma gave me was so much more than Kool-Aid and vocabulary words. They gave me hope. The Zaengleins eventually moved permanently to Florida, and I never saw them again. Charlie passed over in 1963 at the age of eighty, and Emma in 1974, at age ninety-three.

Third grade was a nightmare for me from a human standpoint. My teacher looked and acted like my mother, and we took an immediate dislike to each other. I acted up constantly and was always in trouble for both real and imagined crimes. I spent many afternoons in the principal's office. Although I pretended not to care, I was miserable. Previously an excellent student, my grades plummeted. Depression, especially in children, was not widely recognized in the 1950s, but it is apparent now that I was depressed. By the time I entered the fourth grade, I was in deep emotional trouble, which my new teacher, Helen George, recognized.

She immediately stepped in to help. Many students feared Mrs. George because she was a serious no-nonsense teacher. I loved her. She took a special interest in me from the very beginning and helped me turn both my academic and personal lives around. My grades went from C's to B's to A's and with each human victory, she encouraged me to try harder to reach higher goals. She instilled in me a love of learning that I have never lost and helped me understand that I have worth.

Several years ago when one of the local newspapers ran a profile article on Mrs. George because of her many years of service to the community through various civic organizations, I took the opportunity to write her a note congratulating her on the article and thanking her for all she did for me as a child. I told her about the book I was writing and her inclusion in it. Mrs. George immediately called to thank me. She was not at all impressed by her own accomplishments, but she was thrilled that one of her former students was writing a book. She, of course, had no idea of the impact she had on my young life. I am enormously grateful that I had the opportunity to tell Mrs. George what she meant to me because she is not here, at least in body, to read the book. A few weeks after our conversation, Helen George passed over. She was ninety.

Jeannie Friend was one of my best friends in junior high and high school. Her mother Billie also took a special interest in me. While my parents always dropped me off at Sunday school and church, Jeannie attended every Sunday with her family. I liked being dropped off at church because I almost always sat with Jeannie and her parents, pretending they were my family. Afterward, they would invite me to lunch at Lyman's Restaurant a wonderful old cafeteria in downtown Wapakoneta where I was allowed to order prime rib. I relished this time with what I considered to be a real family. I, of course, didn't understand that I chose my parents for the specific lessons we could learn together. I was always amazed that Billie not only enjoyed being around her own children, Jeannie and David, but also me. She talked to us as adults and asked our opinions of current events. Jeannie and David were less than thrilled for this parental intrusion into their lives, but I thought it was wonderful. My own family chose such a dysfunctional experience that we never talked about anything. Not since Charlie Zaenglein took me under his wing had an adult been interested in my opinion. When I graduated from high school, Billie wrote letters to help me earn scholarships for college. When her husband retired, he and Billie left Wapakoneta. They now divide their time between homes in Michigan and Florida. I am still in touch with her.

Marjorie Flinn Gratz was another woman who had a major impact on my life. I met Marjorie when I was dating her son in high school. He and I chose an interesting contract together in that we liked each other a great deal, but unfortunately never at the same time. When I was crazy about him, he wasn't interested, and by the time he finally decided he wanted me, I was dating someone else. While the relationship with her son was brief, Marjorie was a part of my life for many years. She was a beautiful woman, probably in her mid-forties at the time, who seemed to glow with love and goodness.

Marjorie lived in a small mobile home with her son and his two younger sisters. When I met her, she had recently divorced her abusive husband, the father of her four children. Even though they had almost no money, the home was filled with love. Her son and I were no longer dating by the time he graduated from high school and joined the Navy, which was wonderful for me because I was able to spend almost all my free time with Marjorie and the girls. Possibly the most nurturing woman I had ever met, she welcomed me into her family and accepted me as one of her own. I believe Marjorie and I had experienced other lives together because there was an instant connection between us.

I don't know how my mother felt about my relationship with Marjorie. However, she was insanely jealous when it came to my father. When I asked him to do some minor plumbing work on the tiny house Marjorie had purchased in Lima, she thanked him by sending flowers with a note that read "In appreciation." My mother flew into a rage and wrote a letter to me in which she said, "Dear Marjorie's card and flowers to Leo is [sic] a real gem. 'In appreciation' for what? What has he done for her, with her, or to her?" She concluded the letter by saying: "Whenever you want to come home to see your darling father, or you two want to get together, I won't interfere. I'll stay with Grandma and be out of your way completely." She signed the letter "Someone You Used to Know." I, of course, don't know what my father told Mother about the incident. He may well have said something to promote her rage. That was one of the aspects of our contracts together.

Marjorie eventually remarried, and moved with her husband and the girls to a small town in Indiana. We stayed in touch for several years, but because my relationship with her son ended badly when he came home from the Navy engaged to someone else, I never saw Marjorie again.

The most significant mentor in my life was David Ullery, a Lutheran minister who came to Wapakoneta when I was in the sixth grade. I began counseling with him almost as soon as he arrived. He taught me early on to always look for the humor and irony in any situation.

A rather short man with a cherubic face and casual intensity, Dave was truly a godsend. I instinctively knew that I could trust him—that no matter what I told him, he would continue to love me. Unconditional love was a concept I could scarcely comprehend because that was not what my immediate family chose to experience. I could talk to Dave about the relationship I chose with my mother, and together we would find a thread of humor among the tales of verbal and emotional abuse I agreed to experience. When I became sexually active at sixteen, I could talk to him. He didn't offer approval, only acceptance.

I didn't remember my sacred contract with my father, but I realize now that Dave at least suspected that I chose sexual abuse. He always encouraged me to take responsibility for my life and not be a victim. He told me many times that it doesn't accomplish anything to give people the answers to their problems, because their inexperience deprives them of the benefit of perspective. He emphasized that we can neither solve anyone else's problems nor can we save them. Our journeys to discover our spiritual being are solo. We have to either learn or not learn our lessons on our own. The choice is ours. All anyone can do for another is plant the seeds and wait for them to grow. Dave called that special moment when we finally understand the lesson an "aha!" Over the years he planted a lot of seeds that later sprouted along my path on this earthwalk.

Dave moved to a larger church in Worthington, a suburb of Columbus. Even though I saw him only sporadically after that, he continued to have a profound impact on my life. Dave passed over from kidney dis-ease in 1996, when he was just sixty-three, but even now he continues to guide me. Dave frequently shows up in psychic readings with encouragement, letting me know that he is around me.

With the possible exception of Dave, I doubt if any of these wonderful people had even an inkling of the impact our sacred contracts together had on my earthwalk, and they would probably never consider what they did for me to be extraordinary. They were just kind, loving beings, but I will never forget them.

4
Nobody Will Ever Love Me Like My Daddy Does

When a soul chooses to learn the lessons of being a victim, the Universe provides the scenarios that become the dramas in which the souls perform. Each time the soul misses an opportunity, the Universe will provide another until it finally makes the empowering choice. The result for me was a pattern of dysfunctional relationships with men in which I always found a way to become the victim.

My very first boyfriend, a boy I will call "Rocky," came on the scene when I was in the seventh grade. He lasted through the beginning of my freshman year of high school. A stubborn young man who chose a lifetime with a quick temper and alot of unresolved anger, he was prone to picking fist fights with almost anyone.

Rocky and I didn't have a lot in common, except a penchant for sitting in the back of the local movie theater and necking. After dating a couple of years, I allowed him to feel my breasts. I didn't really mind if Rocky touched my breasts, but I wanted to dump him without having to take responsibility. I told Dave Ullery what Rocky had done "to me," and he, of course, insisted that I end the relationship with Rocky. Rocky was history and I was off the hook.

As he walked me home from school, I gave him the news.

"I have to break up with you."

"What do you mean you have to break up with me? Why? Are you angry about something? Did I do something wrong?" he asked, clearly confused.

"I told my minister that you felt my breasts, and he said we're getting too serious. He said I have to break up with you."

"Why would you tell him something like that? Besides, I thought you liked it."

"I did like it, but Pastor Ullery says we have to break up."

"That's the stupidest thing I've ever heard. Why should we break up just because some guy says we have to? Don't you like me anymore?"

"Sure, I like you, but if I let you feel my breasts, we're going to go further, and I'm afraid I'll end up pregnant. I can't risk it."

"That's crazy!"

"I don't care. We have to break up."

At first glance, it would appear that I was once again a victim because Dave Ullery "forced" me to end a relationship with a boy I really liked. The reality, of course, is that I set the stage for being a victim in the drama when I told Dave that Rocky touched my breasts. I knew what he would say, so rather than take responsibility for wanting to end the relationship with Rocky, I relinquished my power to Dave so that I could be the victim.

I began dating "Apollo" the summer before our sophomore year of high school. Apollo was a nice young man, the first real love of my life, and for more than thirty years, the boy to whom I believed I had lost my virginity in the front seat of his '64 Chevy on the little road beside the local rendering plant.

Petrified of becoming pregnant, I insisted that we needed to use some form of birth control. This was 1966 and options were not only limited but also not easy to come by. Girls had no options at all. The "pill" had not yet made its way to Wapakoneta, and even if it had, an unmarried teenaged girl would never have had access to it. Condoms were sold only in pharmacies and from vending machines in men's rooms at gas stations. I obviously couldn't go to the men's room, and if I had attempted to buy condoms at a pharmacy, the pharmacist would have immediately called my parents. The consequences for most girls would have been almost as unpleasant as an unwanted pregnancy. Boys generally did not like to wear condoms, which in those days were thick and ill-fitting. Most boys likened them to taking a shower with a raincoat on. When I asked my father to get me some sort of birth control, he readily agreed, as I knew he would.

"I told my dad we needed some kind of birth control, and he got me something. It's called foam, and you just put it up there before you have sex." I thought Apollo would be pleased, but I was wrong. Apollo was horrified.

"What do you mean you told your dad? Why would you do that? What's he going to think of me now? And what is this foam stuff? I've never even heard of it."

"I thought you'd be happy. We agreed we wouldn't have sex anymore unless we used some kind of protection. I don't want to get pregnant. Besides, my dad was cool about it. He wouldn't give me something that wasn't going to work." Like so many bizarre events in the life I chose, I didn't even realize that it was unusual to ask, nor did I question how I knew my dad would gladly provide birth control for us when most fathers would have killed the boy and carted the daughter off to a convent for having sex. Our contract was certainly interesting.

To add to the drama, no sooner had I become sexually active than my periods became irregular, which is common in souls who have chosen to experience sexual abuse. Every time I had sex, my period would be late or worse yet, not come at all. I automatically assumed I was pregnant.

In 1966, with abortion being illegal, there were very few options if a girl became pregnant out-of-wedlock. One option was that she would gain some weight caused by a mysterious ailment such as kidney problems. She would go away to a "clinic" for a few months only to return once again thin and presumably cured, having passed an approximately seven pound kidney stone. It was certainly never discussed, even among the closest of friends, because no "decent" boy would date a girl who wasn't virginal. If word got out that a girl had a baby, she would be ostracized forever.

The most common choice was that these two young kids would be forced to get married, which carried a stigma that in small-town Ohio would last for years. No one would have understood a sacred contract. College would be out of the question, and in Apollo's case, a fine athlete, he would have been forced to pass up an athletic scholarship and possibly face life in a low-paying job. There were no good choices. Those fears coupled with my potentially crazy father who was not only willing but eager to provide birth control for his teenage daughter made it all too weird. We were both miserable, Apollo because he had hooked up with a family of probable lunatics who could potentially ruin his life, and me because I could feel him withdrawing from the relationship. Hearing my mother's words echoing in my ears, I knew that if I didn't marry Apollo, my prospects for ever dating another "decent" boy were very slim. I became clingy and emotionally needy, a victim, which caused Apollo to back away even faster. It was all more than poor Apollo could handle and we broke up without any assistance from Dave Ullery.

Even that wasn't enough drama for me. Instead of moving on, I pined for Apollo for years and let everyone know I would never get over him, but, of course, I did. Again I set up the perfect drama to become the victim.

It was 1968, and I was casually dating a quiet, funny boy I'll call "FloJoe." A natural athlete, FloJoe was known for his incredible running speed. We began dating in the early spring of my senior year of high school. It was nothing serious, just the occasional movie or whatever we did in those days. I remember that we laughed a lot and just generally had fun together.

One weekend in May, FloJoe's parents were out of town. He was alone in the house, which could mean only one of two things: invite a girl over and hope to get lucky, or invite the guys over for a drunken party. Unfortunately, in FloJoe's case, his reach exceeded his grasp, and he attempted to do both on the same night.

We had been dating a while, and I liked him. Although we hadn't had sex yet, I'm sure were both excited at the prospect of having our first time be in a real bed rather than a car. His parents being out of town provided just that opportunity.

FloJoe picked me up for our date and drove me to his house, where he produced a bottle of cherry vodka and two glasses. He poured the vodka, and we drank it, glass after glass. What neither of us realized is that I can't hold my liquor. I will go from seemingly sober to falling-down drunk in a matter of seconds with almost no warning.

So FloJoe poured that one glass too many and I was sick. He

helped me stagger to the bathroom where I vomited sickly sweet vodka for what seemed like hours before I mercifully passed out on his bathroom floor. I have no idea how long I was unconscious, but to FloJoe, who was on a tight schedule, it must have seemed like an eternity.

When I came to I was partially lying on a bed, which was right off the kitchen near the back door. My back and upper body were on the bed with my legs hanging over the side. I was wearing only my bra and panties. FloJoe was wearing his white Jockey briefs and white gym socks. He was on top of me obviously trying to finish as quickly as possible. At some point I was bound to regain consciousness and realize something was amiss. I can almost hear Ricky Ricardo's voice echoing in my ear saying, "Oh, Luuucy, you got a lotta esplanin' to do." Only in this case, FloJoe was Lucy.

Unfortunately, the sex part is not what roused me from my drunken stupor. It was the pounding on the glass-topped back door in the kitchen a few feet away where the party guys were peering in, witnessing the scene on the bed.

FloJoe leapt from the bed, picked me up and literally propped me up in the closet of the bedroom because I was still far too drunk to stand. He apparently put my clothes back on me as easily as he had removed them; I was in no condition to assist him. Both finally dressed, FloJoe flung my arm over his shoulder and sort of dragged me, feet barely touching the ground, past the crowd of young men who were by this time doubled over with laughter.

The alcoholic stupor at that moment was a blessing, because I had not yet realized what was happening or that I would have to face these same boys at school on Monday. Instead, trying to wave, I flapped a drunken hand in their general direction and called out cheerfully, "Hi boys!" as FloJoe got me into his car and back to my house.

The next day when I realized what had happened, I was mortified. I was never actually angry with FloJoe. He was undoubtedly drunk too, not unconscious like me, but probably enough that his judgment was impaired. If not, he surely would have removed the ridiculous white socks before engaging in sex. He had a plan. Pick me up. Get drunk. Have sex. Take me home. The guys come, and they have a party. It probably would have worked if I had not passed out and thrown the schedule off. In his alcohol-soaked mind he was just proceeding as planned. The guys would be showing up any minute. He had to hurry and finish before they arrived. I can see exactly what he was thinking and how it happened. If the boys had not shown up, and I would have awakened to find that FloJoe had started without me, I would have laughed.

Instead I was too embarrassed to go back to school on Monday, so I feigned illness and stayed home the whole week. I was so convincing that I spent several of those days in the hospital with mysterious abdominal pain that resulted in a lower GI series all to avoid a little embarrassment. Eventually I had to go back to take my finals, and when I did, no one even mentioned the incident at FloJoe's. At worst there may have been a few knowing smiles and a couple of giggles, but by and large, nothing. I chose to be humiliated because someone saw me having sex, and I didn't want the stigma of being a "bad" girl. For thirty years whenever I told the story, the boys were pointing and jeering after witnessing FloJoe raping me. When I finally went back to school, it was even worse with the girls also joining in. It might actually have been what I believed.

The Universe provided a powerful opportunity for me to step out of my familiar victim role and take responsibility for my actions. Instead I chose to stay with the comfortable and play the victim simply because my human ego was embarrassed.

5
But it Was Such a Good Band

It was always whispered throughout the community, among students and parents alike, that the band director had a penchant for fondling young girls.

The touching began innocently enough when a young girl, usually in fifth or sixth grade, received private instruction from the director. Typically, he would begin by helping the young girl learn to breathe correctly from the diaphragm. He would place his arm around the girl's waist as she played her instrument and press her diaphragm to make sure she was breathing properly. At the same time, he would help her keep time by tapping the rhythm on her knee with his other hand. Suddenly his hand would brush her breast very gently. It was so subtle that the first few times it happened she would assume it was a mistake, an accident. She would even question whether or not it had actually happened or if it was just her imagination. After several weeks, she would realize that it was no accident, but what could she do? No one would believe her. It would be her word against his. So she remained silent, hoping the touching would stop, but, of course, it never did.

That was the way it began with me and many other young girls over the years. We didn't openly discuss what was happening, and we certainly didn't understand that this was part of our sacred contract with the band director. At that time, girls didn't discuss sex with their friends even if they were in serious relationships with steady boyfriends, because no one wanted the stigma of being a "bad" girl.

More importantly, we feared that no one would believe us, and we would end up in a lot of trouble. By the time it had gone on for several years, we felt it was too late. Why, they would ask, didn't we come forward sooner? Obviously, they would conclude that it had been consensual, and from the spiritual standpoint, it was. From the human standpoint, however, it was a nightmare for countless young women for years.

For me it was not a nightmare, but more of an annoyance. Souls who have chosen to experience sexual abuse frequently display an array of specific characteristics in their human lives including difficulty in establishing boundaries with men. Almost every boy I ever went out with tried to feel my breasts. To me it was not a big deal. I considered asking the band director to stop, but I felt, since it was so subtle, he would deny he was intentionally touching me. I knew the touching would stop if I said something, but I feared retribution. The man had a temper, prone to screaming and throwing objects at students.

My future husband Dan had a short-lived band career that ended abruptly when the director yelled at another student and threw a blackboard eraser that whizzed by Dan's ear, striking the cymbal next to him. Instinctively Dan threw his drumstick back at the director and walked out.

As long as I kept quiet, the director didn't pick on me, and in fact I was one of his "pets." The touching was not important enough for me to jeopardize my special status. I'm not certain I even understood his touching would be considered abuse by human standards. It was just annoying.

Finally though, when I was a junior, the touching became more blatant. One day he came up behind me, slid his hands underneath my pink angora sweater, and grabbed both my breasts. A few days later at one of my private lessons, he slid his hand all the way up my skirt. Even then I was not frightened, but he had crossed a line where I was not willing to go. I knew if I didn't tell someone, it was likely his behavior would escalate further.

I decided to tell my father. He was on the board of education at the time, so the superintendent had to respond. He questioned me for what seemed like an eternity. He asked that I recount every incident I could remember, over and over in detail, looking for discrepancies in my story, and as I spoke, he interrupted me repeatedly with questions. How many years had this been going on? Why hadn't I ever told anyone before? My answer was always that I was afraid. In reality though, I couldn't dispute anything the superintendent said. I didn't know about sacred contracts, but I knew that I had allowed the touching to go on for years. I felt guilty for turning the director in even though in human terms, it was the right thing to do.

Finally the superintendent asked me if there was anyone else who could corroborate my story. There were whispers and rumors, but as teenagers, no one actually discussed the fondling. I was only guessing when I nervously gave the superintendent the names of two girls who I believed might have also been fondled by the director. Then I prayed that they would have the courage to tell the truth.

Fortunately, when their turns came to be questioned, both girls told stories similar to mine. If the girls had been too frightened to tell the truth or if I had chosen two girls who had not been touched, my band career would certainly have been over, and I would likely have been ostracized.

The board and superintendent were forced to act. The band director was called before them but, instead of being fired, he was allowed to resign. He left the school not as someone who had agreed to be a pedophile in this earthwalk, but as a hero. They dedicated the yearbook to him. Many people in Wapakoneta still revered him. Even in his nineties, whenever this former band director came through town, word would spread and a crowd of former students would gather at a local restaurant where he would meet with them.

My reaction was interesting, but still typical of someone choosing to be a victim. Even though turning him in was courageous in human terms, when the man didn't leave in disgrace I felt even guiltier. Suddenly the story became embellished. I was horrified when he touched me, and terrified that he was going to rape me. I added as much drama as possible to enhance my level of victimization because I chose to feel guilty.

Once more the Universe presented me with the opportunity for empowerment and courage, but instead of taking responsibility for my actions that in human terms were correct. I again chose to be a victim. Since I was not traumatized by the touching itself, I became a victim by assuming guilt for reporting him.

6
And Then
I Killed Harley

I was a junior in high school when I first met the boy I will call Harley Clearwater because his two loves in life were motorcycles and rock and roll. It seemed that whenever we had a class together, he sat either directly in front of me or behind me. He was dating a good friend of mine, so even though there was an instant chemistry between us, we didn't pursue it. Instead, we would flirt and play tricks on each other. I would write messages such as "bite me" on the back of his neck, and he, pretending to be furious, would scribble on my notebooks. Of course it was kid stuff, but we were kids.

When he and my friend broke up, he asked me out. Homecoming was our first "official" date, and I was really excited about going with Harley. He was fun and easy to be around, the first boy I was ever comfortable talking with. When I opened the front door and saw him standing there looking so handsome in his suit, smiling and holding a corsage for me, my heart melted. I was wearing a short navy dress that would have gotten me expelled were it not homecoming, so I imagine he was pleased as well. We had fun together, laughing and talking and as he brought me home, sharing our first kiss.

We dated on and off the rest of the school year. Neither of us was interested in a monogamous relationship. Frequently he just showed up. Occasionally he made a date and then didn't show up because he would be hustling some guy in pool or playing cards to win money for the date. Finally, the night after graduation, after an evening of drinking at various parties, we found ourselves back at my house. It was late and my parents were gone for the night. We had been making out heavily, both excited, when Harley stammered, "Uh, I was wondering if maybe you wanted to do it. I have a condom."

"Do I want to *do it?*" I asked.

"Yeah. Do you want to do it?" he asked.

"Sure." He was so cute and so nervous that I couldn't resist. Besides I had wanted to "do it" with him since the moment I met him.

"You will?!" His surprise and fear were evident in his voice.

"Yeah."

"Oh man! I didn't think you'd do it!"

"Then why did you ask me?"

"Well, I kind of hoped that you would, but I didn't think, I mean…"

I was finally ready to commit to him, ready for a serious, monogamous relationship, and I was equally certain that he felt the same way. It was definitely love.

Two weeks passed and I didn't hear from him. I was surprised, but not yet devastated. He didn't date much, so I wasn't overly concerned, just mildly annoyed. When I finally ran into him, he was with someone else. I couldn't believe it! Now I was devastated!

Instead of getting angry, I slipped into my best victim mode. How could I have been so stupid? How could I let him use me like that? I really liked Harley. I didn't want him to use me. I wanted him to love me. Harley, on the other hand, was just an ornery, thrill-seeking kid who had no intention of getting serious with anyone.

I didn't see him the rest of the summer, but he called the night before I left for Ohio University to begin my freshman year. He would be leaving for Ohio State a few days later.

"Listen, this is Harley. I'm really sorry about what happened, and I was wondering if maybe you'd like to go out tomorrow and we could talk.

"I'm leaving tomorrow."

"How about tonight then?" he asked.

"I have to pack," I said and I hung up. That was the end of that, I thought. A few fun times, and now it was time to move on. I'd go away to school—that cute Dan Fischer was at OU—and forget all about Harley and his dimples. Of course, things rarely work out the way we plan because we don't remember our sacred contracts.

I did go to OU, but the relationship with Harley was far from over. I was happily entrenched in life at OU, involved in the fledgling anti-war and women's movements, and even enjoying my classes. Then I saw a tiny article in the Wapakoneta Daily News under the heading "College News." It said simply that Harley Clearwater was a freshman at Ohio State and that he would enjoy hearing from his friends, and then it listed his address.

"Dear Harley," my letter began. "I don't know if I would classify us as friends, but whatever, I would enjoy hearing from people I know too." The letter was casual and newsy with nothing personal and no mention of anything that had happened between us in the past.

Harley wrote back immediately: "The minute I saw the handwriting on the envelope I knew the letter was from you. I couldn't wait to rip it open. You were the last person on earth I expected to hear from after the way I treated you and all, but I'm sure glad you wrote." He talked about school. "I'm taking ROTC. Listen, this is the biggest piece of shit in the world because these guys treat us like new inductees, screaming orders at us," he wrote. "I look kind of neat in my uniform, though, except for the pants which flap my legs black and blue when I'm in the wind. You have to salute all these guys with round hats and red patches and I sort of get a kick out of it."

It wasn't until much later that I would realize the irony of my marching against the war at the same time he was marching as part of the military establishment.

Then he began to apologize, and he was obviously sincere at least at the moment he wrote it. "I'm really sorry for the way I treated you. There was no excuse for it, just not calling you and all, and I wouldn't blame you if you never spoke to me again. I hope you will though, and I hope you'll go out with me again. I'll make it up to you, I promise, and I'll never treat you that way again. So please come home at Thanksgiving, and we'll go out. OK? Now that I've said all that, I think I have to take a sedative and lie down."

Of course, I went home at Thanksgiving, and we went out

several times over the break. We had so much fun together that I could barely wait for the longer Christmas holiday to see him again.

When we went back to school after Christmas and I missed a period, I immediately thought I was pregnant. I wrote Harley and gave him the news. He didn't take it well.

"Look," he wrote back. "You know I'm willing to use protection anytime, but it's up to you to let me know when it's safe. I don't have any way of knowing when it's safe or not. There's no way in hell I'm ready to get married or have a baby. What are we going to do?"

"Don't worry about it. If I'm pregnant, I'll take care of it." It was a bold statement, considering that abortion wasn't legal, and I had no idea how to go about getting one, but, of course, victims love drama.

When I discovered I wasn't pregnant as we had feared, we were both relieved, but the tension between us was noticeable. We had dodged a bullet, but it was a scary time for both of us. Although we continued to write and called occasionally, we didn't see each other until March when we both came home. We went out as usual, and then we came back to my house.

"I think I'm just using you for sex. I thought I should tell you," he said.

"Oh, stop it! You're not using me. You're upset about the pregnancy scare. I was upset too. It was really scary, but we got through it and we won't be so careless anymore. It will be fine."

"Yeah, but I know I don't want to get married for a long time. I think maybe I'm just using you."

I immediately burst into tears

Harley was the first boy I *didn't* feel was using me for sex, and now he was telling me he was. I knew he was merely upset, but I was a victim, and so I chose to be devastated.

"Oh, God. Please don't cry. I didn't mean to hurt your feelings. I would never hurt your feelings. I only meant…"

"Get out! Just get out of my house!"

I went back to school, and in typical victim fashion, sank into a depression so deep that I took a bottle of nonprescription sleeping pills. I don't know if I intended to die, but I'm sure I thought suicide would make Harley feel horrible for treating me so badly. As suicide attempts go, this one was fairly feeble. It was better than the time I took prescription allergy medicine and instead of dying just had really dry nasal passages for about a week, but not much better. This time my roommates found me groggy but conscious. When I told them what I had done, they assured me that no man, especially Harley, was worth dying for. I refused to let them take me to the college health center, which was notorious for its poor care. I felt it was far more dangerous to my health than the pills I had swallowed. They managed to force me to vomit, and then let me sleep for two days. I didn't seem to suffer any ill effects, and came out of the experience with a new determination never to speak to Harley again.

After a couple of weeks with no communication from me, Harley wrote. He tried to be casual, as though nothing had happened. When I didn't respond, he wrote again. "I was just sitting here thinking about why you haven't written. I hope it isn't because of what I said. I didn't want to hurt your feelings. I just thought I should be honest about how I felt. I'm just not ready to get married or take care of a baby."

Again, I didn't respond. He kept writing, with each letter becoming more desperate and depressed than the one before. He had, for the most part, stopped studying or going to class, and he was drinking heavily with his buddies on a nightly basis. He was clearly in trouble, but I wasn't about to intervene.

Though I read each of his letters, I never responded. We were falling into what was to become a familiar pattern in how we responded to our relationship. I withdrew emotionally, and he engaged in some sort of reckless, potentially self-destructive behavior. Although we didn't know it, it was our sacred contract. We were co-dependent victims.

He continued writing, sometimes a couple of times a week, but now in addition to everything else, he was talking about enlisting in the Army. We were in the middle of the Vietnam War; everyone else we knew was doing anything they could to avoid being drafted, and he was talking about enlisting.

His normally small, concise handwriting was becoming large and sprawling. I knew he was depressed, but I still refused to write him. In the meantime, I began dating a nice young man from the Columbus area. We were in the same speech class, and he called after I gave a rousing speech in favor of the Vietnam War. The assignment was to give a controversial speech, and since I was involved in the anti-war movement, I couldn't think of anything more controversial, at least on a personal level, than a pro-war stance. He missed the irony altogether and thought he had found a kindred spirit. He was conservative, in a fraternity, and everything that I was not. I was too depressed to care. I was a victim on the rebound, and he was handsome and a nice guy. I was glad to have a steady boyfriend to take my mind off Harley and his rapid downward spiral. Harley wasn't my problem, I told myself. He had brought all of this on himself. I didn't care what happened to him. I was the victim, not him.

The semester ended. The day I got home for the summer, Harley called. "I'm glad you're home. May I come over?"

"No. I'm dating someone else."

"Oh. Is it OK if I come over?"

"No."

When I hung up the phone I took a shower and changed my clothes. I knew he would be over. He was. The doorbell rang, and there he stood, dimples and all.

"I'm going down to volunteer for the draft tomorrow. That way it will only be two years instead of the four if I actually enlisted. I already talked to them. They said I won't have to leave until late August. We can spend the whole summer together."

"There is no 'we.' I'm going with someone else now. But Jesus, Harley, when did you become so gung ho? This is insane! Just get back in school somewhere and wait it out. If you go into the Army you'll end up in Vietnam. If you go over there, you'll get your damned head blown off! I know you! Just stay in school one more year, and maybe it will be over by then." I couldn't understand how he could be so stupid.

"You don't understand," he said. "I have to go. It's a matter of honor. Besides, I'm so confused, I don't have a clue what I want to do with my life. Maybe by the time I get out I'll have it figured out."

"Yeah, and maybe by the time you get out, you'll be dead! Honor? What the hell are you talking about honor? Where's the honor in killing innocent women and children?" I knew it was point-less talking to him, because he was determined to go.

We were together every day the rest of the summer until he

shipped out in late August. By the time he left, I had decided not to return to college. In all the turmoil of the preceding months, I hadn't gotten a real job for the summer. Now I realized I was low on money because my job selling encyclopedias door-to-door turned out not to be as lucrative as one might imagine. I decided to move to Columbus, get an apartment and a job, and maybe take a few night classes.

As soon as Harley shipped out I immediately moved, scrounging whatever furnishings I could from family and friends. My first sofa and matching chair were maroon mohair, with cushions that sank to the floor when anyone sat on them. I didn't care. I was just happy to be on my own.

I landed my first job as a clerk typist for a large insurance company. It wasn't a great job, but then I was neither a great clerk nor a great typist, so it was an equitable relationship.

Dave and Beth Ullery had just moved to Worthington, a suburb of Columbus, and my best friend, Joerdie and her fiancé, Eric, who were getting married in a few weeks, were also there while he finished school. Even though I missed Harley terribly, I had a good support system.

I wrote Harley almost daily. My life wasn't that exciting, since I didn't have much money to go out with my friends, and I was trying to save enough to go back to school. Consequently, my letters were long on style and short on substance, but he was grateful for any mail I sent. He wrote at least once a week; his letters were funny and exciting. He loved basic training and viewed each new experience as an adventure.

Harley was smart and he was fearless, sometimes to the point of recklessness. In those days, when there were deferments for college and other things, draftees were frequently poorly educated and unmotivated because they weren't there voluntarily. Harley was exactly what the Army was looking for.

"I signed up for Airborne Jump School and just got word that I was accepted. I talked to my platoon sergeant and he said that the people who were accepted for Jump School will get a chance to get stationed almost anywhere at one of the Army's overseas bases—especially 'Nam. He said 90% of all airborne personnel volunteer for 'Nam. I volunteered at my interview to go over, so it's almost definite I'll go. I can't wait. Hope I can get with the 101st Screaming Eagles division."

I didn't tell him at that point how insane I thought it was for him to have volunteered. It was already done, and I didn't think there was anything he could do about it.

Harley and I had a great Christmas together. When his leave was over, he headed to Airborne training. As with every new adventure, Harley loved it. When he graduated a few weeks later, he got the news we had been expecting.

"Well, in a few more days I'll be home. We graduated yesterday after our 5th jump. Had ceremonies on the drop zone. Jumped yesterday with about 200 lbs. of equipment and I thought my shoulders were broken 'til I got out of the plane. I'll tell you what, going airborne is the greatest experience I've ever completed with my clothes on! Well, anyway, halfway through graduation, the director of the Airborne department told us that 103 of us were scheduled to be replacements for the 173rd Airborne Unit in Vietnam. Right now I'm at Headquarters Company waiting to start my out processing tomorrow morning. I should be home Tuesday or Wednesday."

Harley came home on Wednesday. I made arrangements to take the rest of the week off to be with him. We went out that first night, and before he left, we had a serious misunderstanding. It really was a misunderstanding, not a fight; there was no anger. The specific details only marginally add to the story. It is sufficient to say it was a serious misunderstanding, but not so serious that we wouldn't have resolved it if we had more time. Unfortunately, we were out of time.

I was home until Sunday before heading back to Columbus, but Harley didn't call. Another week of his three-week leave passed and he still hadn't called. A girl who had always been my nemesis in high school because we had a penchant for dating the same boys, called to tell me that Harley had been in Columbus over the weekend with a group of guys. Angry and insecure, I took the bait and called him. Even though I knew what was really bothering him, I was still angry that Harley would come to Columbus, where I lived, and not even call.

In 1970, women generally didn't call men, and Harley, being more than a little macho, didn't like that I had taken it upon myself to call him. I called him anyway. He was no doubt hung over and probably asleep, neither of which did anything to improve his mood.

"So I heard you were in Columbus over the weekend. Why didn't you call?"

"I was busy."

"Too damn busy to pick up the phone and call?"

"Yeah."

"Fine. You've got another ten days before you ship out. I won't be coming home or calling you again unless I hear from you. If you want to see me, you're going to have to call me." I was in full victim mode.

"Fine."

Fine. That was it, the last time I ever talked with him. Already upset by our misunderstanding, and angry about my ultimatum, he didn't call. The week passed and he left. We had both retreated into our familiar patterns of being victims that were part of our sacred contracts. I withdrew from the relationship, and he became reckless. This time, however, he was in a war zone.

Shortly after Harley shipped out I saw an article in the Wapakoneta paper with his name and address, saying that he would like to hear from his friends. It was similar to the one I answered when we were in college, only this time I didn't respond.

Then the first letter arrived.

"Well, as of today, I've been in this God-forsaken place one month. Twelve more to go. Look, I know you're pissed off because I didn't call you," he wrote. "To tell you the truth that three weeks flew by so fast, I don't even know where it went. Yeah, I should have called you, but it's too late now. I'm sorry. I'm begging you though to please write me. Even if you only want to be my friend, I can understand that, but please write me."

I wrote him back and told him the only commitment I was willing to make was to agree to be there when he got home, not involved in a serious relationship with anyone else. We continued writing at least once a week, and the relationship was soon back to normal.

In each of his letters, Harley described in graphic detail the horrors of war and what he was experiencing. From the human perspective it was frightening, because he had gone from being a happy, thrill-seeking kid to an angry, bitter man in a few short months, but, of course, we didn't understand he agreed to this experience long before he enlisted.

Then the phone call came, the one I had been dreading. Harley was dead. Before his parents could contact me, his neighbor called to say that she had seen two soldiers in full dress uniform going into his house. There was nothing else it could mean.

I happened to be at my parents home that weekend when my dad answered the phone. I could tell from his end of the conversation that whatever had occurred was serious and that it probably involved death.

"Are you sure? Are you sure?" he kept asking. "OK. Thanks for calling."

"Did Uncle Carl die?" I asked casually. Uncle Carl had been having health problems, so his passing would not have been a total surprise nor would it have been especially traumatic, at least for me.

I'll never forget my dad's face, drawn and drained of color; he seemed to have aged ten years during that thirty-second conversation. He looked down, shook his head, and said softly. "Harley."

It took several seconds for me to slip into full victim mode. In those seconds I went from casual interest in Uncle Carl's untimely passing to the horrible realization that Harley was dead. It seemed like an eternity. I opened my mouth to scream, but the only sound to emerge was a low guttural moan, like a wounded animal. I ran from the kitchen, sobbing hysterically, and began frantically packing to go back to Columbus. My father stopped me.

"You can't leave. You're too upset to drive. You'll have an accident, and you'll be dead too. I wouldn't be able to live with that."

"That's exactly what I want!" I screamed, and of course, it was. I was a victim, and this was the role of a lifetime. How could I possibly go on living without Harley? He was my life; at least he became my life the moment I knew he was gone.

What I remember most about the next few weeks is the gnawing emptiness I felt in the pit of my stomach with the realization that I would never see him again. I not only didn't believe I could survive, I didn't believe I deserved to survive. Obviously, my refusal to write him after he didn't call directly caused his death just as my refusal to write him caused him to flunk out of college and go to Vietnam in the first place. For a helpless victim, I had exhibited an enormous burst of power.

For over thirty years I believed that I caused Harley's death. I never told anyone, not even Dan or Joerdie, because I felt ashamed and guilty. For all those years, I thought he flunked out of college and joined the Army because of me, and then I believed that his depression led to his reckless behavior and ultimately his death. I wish I had that kind of power, but I don't. We're all responsible for our own lives and our own choices. Harley made his own choices, but I lived for thirty years with the guilt I created from believing I had killed him. It was the logical choice for me because the greater my perceived guilt, the greater my opportunity to be a victim.

7
Is Self-Pity
One Word, Or Two?

After Harley was killed, I directed most of my energies toward being a victim. It was what I did best. Guilt is one of the most useless and self-defeating emotions we manifest in our human experience, yet I chose to wallow in it because it allowed me to stay in victim mode.

I was depressed and I was angry, mostly with myself. The only person, it seems, I was not angry with was my father. I would call him from my apartment in Columbus and say, "Hello, Daddy?" before erupting into hysterical sobbing. After about ten minutes of me crying with no other words being spoken, I would say, "I'll talk to you later," and hang up. This went on several times a week for months.

To ensure that I could immerse myself in self-pity as long as possible, I intentionally did not call either Dave Ullery or Joerdie, both of whom were living in Columbus. If I had called, I knew that neither of them would have allowed me to continue on my self-destructive path. They would have insisted I do something positive to help me deal with my grief, which I chose to prolong as long as possible. Instead of seeking out my support system, I plunged down every negative avenue I could find. Never much of a drinker, I turned to drugs and sex. I was certain they would steer me far away from the healthy choices Dave and Joerdie might have tried to force upon me.

I began hanging out with friends who were all recreational drug users. We went to parties almost nightly where there was always plenty of alcohol and drugs and lots of strange people, many eager for sex. I had enough judgment remaining that prevented me from bringing them home, but not enough to prevent me from having sex with some them.

I became involved with two senior salesmen from my office, one very married and the other intermittently married and divorced, making it difficult to keep track of his marital status. I lived in the same apartment complex as the intermittently married one for a short time. We became involved when I naively asked if I could borrow his garden hose to wash my car. He lent me his hose, all right; my car, however, remained dirty!

I was working as the word processing secretary for the IBM office in Columbus, which in large part entailed preparing quotations and other material for the sales staff. Being professional salesmen, they often tried their best pitches on me. I usually just laughed them off. None of the men were overly pushy because they didn't want to jeopardize their jobs. After I killed Harley, I began to accept some of their propositions.

Even though I was only into minor drugs like marijuana and speed, I was doing some sort of drug almost every night. While I usually made it to work, I was often late and always surly. The overall quality of my work was still very good, but getting me to do a particular job took a lot of cajoling. Some days I just closed my door and sobbed. Apparently I was not always subtle. When I would finally emerge with puffy red eyes and splotchy face, I would find a candy bar or a soda that some anonymous person had left to cheer me up. I might have been reprimanded or even fired for my attitude and behavior had I not been bedding the most influential of the sales staff. They protected me from the wrath of the angry young lions who couldn't get their work done because of me. I was also able to sink further into victim mode for allowing these men to "use me." Fortunately this phase was short-lived. It would have no doubt lasted longer had I not taken a turn for the worse.

My life had always been an erratic cycle of highs and lows, but I knew this was different. Instead of getting better, I keep sinking. I was inconsolable, so depressed that I was barely functioning at even the most rudimentary level. Finally I began missing work because I couldn't concentrate enough to even type a simple letter. I had only been at the job with IBM a few months. It was a great job with full benefits. It paid almost 50% more than my job at the insurance company. I couldn't afford to lose it. In 1970 depression was not widely accepted as a valid medical condition. You were told to pull yourself together and just get over it. I called Dr. Welby in Wapakoneta. Without even examining me, he certified to the Company that I had mononucleosis and would need to be off work on near-complete bed rest for a month. I went home to Wapakoneta to recover, not from the imaginary mono, but from the intense grief and guilt I was feeling. I hadn't stayed with my parents for more than a few days at a time since I moved to Columbus. I wasn't certain if any of us could stand it, but I knew I would not survive by myself, alone in my apartment in Columbus, and I had no place else to go.

The four weeks at home were healing, in a peculiar way, and I was actually sorry when they ended. Mother was recovering from back surgery and spent all of her time in bed. The only real contact we had was when I cooked the meals, which I carried in to her, but mostly I spent time with my dad. It was almost surreal. I cooked and cleaned and did his laundry, all the things a good wife would do, except that there was no sexual contact. I had him all to myself, just the way it should be. I was the good wife, and she was the shrew in the other room. Part of our contract included that Mother and I would always be rivals for my dad. When he wasn't working, we did projects together, like building shelves for my apartment where I could house the shrine to St. Harley I was putting together. It wasn't exactly a happy time. I was so deep into victim mode that I knew I would never be happy again, but it was peaceful.

8
Terrible Tim

When I returned to Columbus after the month at home, I was well-rested and my emotions weren't quite so raw, but I was far from stable. Knowing that it was dangerous for me to be alone, I moved to a larger apartment with a girl from work. That's when I met a friend of hers, a boy I refer to as Terrible Tim.

Tim was a talented but volatile and irresponsible artist. There was electricity between us from the moment we met. In fact, after our first night together, he didn't leave for more than a year.

Tim could be a sweet and sensitive boy with a good sense of humor, and we decided to get an apartment of our own after only a couple of months together. No sooner had we moved than a totally different side of Tim emerged. He was jealous and abusive in a way I had never before experienced in a relationship with a man, certainly not with Harley. Tim more than fulfilled my need to suffer. Soon I was no longer permitted to see any of my old friends, at least not without him. It was a moot point, because his behavior was so erratic and unpredictable that I never would have taken him around any of my friends. I didn't know from one minute to the next which Tim would appear, the sweet gentle young man or the verbally and phys-ically abusive one. If I had agreed to experience being a victim, Tim played his role to perfection, and so did I.

Every day it was the same. I would come home from work and Tim would interrogate me about what I had done that day. Who had I talked to? Were there any men? Did I fuck them over my lunch hour? Tim didn't know about my past, and had no reason not to trust me. It was just his nature to be jealous and paranoid in our drama together.

"You're nothing but a fucking pig!" he would scream over and over. "Did you fuck them today? Did you? I know you did! You're just a fucking pig! Look at you! You have a big ass that sticks out in the back and a big gut that sticks out in the front! You're disgusting. You're damn lucky to have me. No one else would ever want you." At the time, I was no more than a size ten.

I would cower in the corner of the dining room or on the sofa, arms raised on either side in protection as he slapped me open-handed about the head and shoulders. It didn't appear that he intended to inflict physical harm, just emotional abuse and humiliation. Then he would tell me how much he loved me and that no one else would ever love me the way he did.

"I love you so much, little baby girl. You know I do. I just can't stand the thought of you with anybody else. Nobody will ever love you the way I do." Obviously, he had never met my father!

I created the ideal victim scenario. Tim didn't pay rent or contribute to any of the household expenses. I supported us both on my secretarial salary, which left me nearly broke. I allowed it so I could complain and be even more of a victim. He used his salary to buy marijuana and alcohol, which he used to excess and which rendered him more jealous and abusive than before. Living alone with him in an apartment, I was further isolated from my friends, which was exactly what Tim wanted and it filled my need to suffer. We rarely saw anyone but each other.

On weekends he would take my car keys, which meant I was without the means to get away in addition to not having any money. I was deeply ensconced in the victim role and playing it to the hilt. Through the whole ordeal, the slapping around, the verbal abuse, I remember thinking to myself, "It isn't always going to be this way. I'm not going to spend the rest of my life like this." Part of me knew even then that it was only a game.

When Tim announced it was time for us to get married, I panicked. I certainly hadn't counted on that! I didn't want to marry this man, to have children with him, but I was deep into the victim role with no discernable power. I allowed him to control me completely because I needed to be punished for killing Harley. We bought wedding bands with my credit card, and made an appointment for blood tests, the last step before a marriage license and ceremony. I cried myself to sleep that night at the prospect of being legally bound to this man for the rest of my life, not the usual reaction of a young bride-to-be. The drama had just about played itself out, because in an uncommon act of defiance, I insisted that I would not allow anyone but Dave Ullery to marry us. When he saw that I would not budge on the issue, Tim reluctantly agreed.

I called Dave, and made an appointment for the three of us to meet on Saturday morning to discuss our wedding plans. When Saturday came, Tim, hung over from a night of drugs and alcohol, refused to get out of bed to go to our appointment. Both embarrassed by Tim's behavior and relieved that I would get to talk with Dave alone, I went to the appointment. No sooner had I walked into his office than I burst into tears and began telling him about life with Tim. As I knew he would, Dave said he would never marry me to such a character and would do everything he could to see that no one else would marry us either. He told me to go home immediately and tell Tim to move out. I did with Tim exactly what I had done with Rocky years earlier. Rather than take responsibility for ending a relationship that had played itself out, I used Dave to do it for me again. The stakes were higher this time because Rocky was a young boy when Dave gave him the boot. He went quietly. I feared Tim wouldn't be so easy.

When I told Tim that Dave refused to marry us, and that I would not be married by anyone else, we had a terrible fight that continued for nearly a week. The next weekend, when I refused to eat at McDonald's, Tim slapped me around much more severely than ever before. It was the final nudge I needed. I told him to take his things and get out. I had tried to get him out several times before during the year we were together, but he would always cry and beg me to let him stay. No victim could resist that, so I relented. This time it didn't work. I was ready to end the drama. I insisted that he pack up and leave.

I expected trouble. At least in our drama together Tim was jealous with a violent temper. I didn't expect him to go quietly. To my amazement, he packed his things and left. As soon as the last of

Tim's things were gone, the landlord installed new locks and the telephone company gave me a new, unlisted number. Both, of course, added to the drama. Tim came back once, couldn't get in, and left in a huff. To my amazement, I never saw him again. Perhaps he wasn't so terrible after all.

While Tim's behavior was certainly abusive from the human standpoint, he was only playing his part in the drama I created. It was a miserable experience, but it was exactly what I chose at that time. A part of me always knew that it was not going to last forever. I ended it when it no longer met my needs. I honor Tim for his willingness to participate. He was a powerful teacher.

Section Three:
I Find Love,
But Not Necessarily
Happiness

9
A Table
And Three Chairs

It was late December, 1971, just before Christmas. I was still on a high from escaping from Tim. The doorbell rang at the old house on Harrison Street, and when I opened it, there stood Dan Fischer, a boy I had been enamored with since the seventh grade. Had I not been feeling fairly good about myself, I wouldn't have had the presence of mind to invite him inside.

This was December, in the days when winter in Ohio meant something, so Dan would not have hung around long on the cold porch. He came in with a small package, a light blue candle covered with a white frosted design. It was a beautiful gift and a lovely gesture, which took me by surprise. Most of the boys I dated came wanting sex; they certainly didn't bear gifts.

Even though I had had a crush on Dan through my entire junior high and high school years, I never told anyone except Joerdie. Junior high was when boys and girls began hanging out together in groups, and that was when I first spotted Dan. I was basically very shy and never would have imagined that someone like Dan—handsome, athletic, and talented—would ever be interested in me. I wasn't about to risk the almost certain rejection.

Instead, when I graduated from high school, I enrolled at Ohio University, where Dan was a sophomore. Although I tell people I was stalking Dan, I actually chose OU because my sister, Peggy, was there and because the school boasted an excellent journalism program. Dan was just an added bonus.

Harley and I had a tumultuous relationship, and even though we were together the better part of three years, there were periods when we were not even speaking, let alone dating. The beginning of my freshman year at OU was one of those times. If I was ever going to snag Dan Fischer, this was my chance. We shared a psychology class, one of those huge lecture classes with hundreds of students and a professor who barely spoke English. I would wait for Dan, just out of sight, and then appear suddenly from seemingly out of nowhere when he arrived for class. Depending on my timing, we would sometimes sit together, but at the very least, I made certain that he saw me and would hopefully think about me for the rest of the day. My plan worked because by early October he asked me out. I was so excited that my roommates and I made a trip to Columbus to find the perfect outfit, an extremely short, tight dress, permanently dubbed my "Danny Fischer dress."

It was Homecoming weekend and he invited me to a Simon and Garfunkel concert. Following the concert, Dan took me to a party at a shack he and his friends had built in a cornfield on the outskirts of Athens. It was two plywood rooms with a crude roof, and enough space between the outside boards for light to shine through. Inside was nothing but numerous old mattresses on the rough wooden floor. Clearly its purpose was drinking, drugs, and sex. Even with only a few weeks of college under my belt, I was well-versed in alcohol and sex, and I found that one usually accompanied the other. That was Dan's hope as he poured paper cup after paper cup of Southern Comfort straight from the bottle. As he made his move to seduce me, I resisted slightly. He was, after all, a "decent" boy and hearing my mother's warnings swirling around in my alcohol-soaked brain about decent boys not dating girls who weren't pure, I didn't want him to think I was a "bad" girl.

We began kissing and soon found ourselves prone on our designated mattress where I'm certain we would have consummated our budding lust. Once horizontal, however, the effects of too much cheap alcohol kicked in and I promptly passed out. Dan Fischer, that decent boy who obviously liked me, would have to wait for another day.

The long drive back to Athens was made even longer by the fact that Dan had to drive very slowly so that I could hang my head out the passenger door and vomit all the way back to town. The relationship was off to a rocky start.

Too embarrassed to face Dan, I dodged his phone calls for several days. I couldn't avoid him forever though, because the car he had driven was mine, and he had the keys. We agreed to meet for dinner at the local BBF, a precursor to McDonald's, and the only fast food-restaurant in town at the time.

"Listen, I'm really embarrassed by the other night," I began. "I guess I should have told you I'm a cheap drunk. If you were going to try to seduce me, you would have been better off using ice cream."

"Yeah, I'm sorry if I offended you. I'm not usually so forward."

We finished our sandwiches and left the restaurant. Taking my hand as we walked down the sidewalk Dan said shyly, "Would you like some ice cream?"

Most of Dan's weekends were filled with band gigs. I hung out with him as a quasi-groupie, but it wasn't a real relationship. By Thanksgiving break we had stopped seeing each other, and Harley and I were back together. I didn't see Dan again until he showed up on my porch with the candle.

So now, years later, Dan was sitting in my living room. What could it mean? I was living in Columbus, Harley was dead, I had just broken up with Tim. How did Dan even know I was in Wapakoneta?

"Someone told me you were in town. I thought I would take a chance that you would still be home."

A good sign, I thought; he sought me out.

Dan had just graduated from Ohio University, a semester later than planned. When the Nixon administration announced the draft lottery system to replace the draft, his number was eight. He was absolutely certain to be called. Always a sensitive kid, Dan worried so much about being forced to go to Vietnam that he developed ulcerative colitis. When the symptoms began, they were severe enough that he had to be hospitalized, ironically by Dr. Welby, who always seemed to play a significant role in our lives. At the same time, college students on campuses across the country began protesting the U.S. invasion of Cambodia as an expansion of the Vietnam War. On May 4, 1970, as Dan lay in a hospital bed in Lima and Harley was in Vietnam fighting, four students at Kent State University were shot and killed by National Guard troops. The violence and ensuing riots escalated to the point where Governor Rhodes closed all of Ohio's state universities until fall. Had Dan been at OU, he would have received credit for all of his classes; instead, he was in the hospital and lost credit for the entire semester. He had to return in the fall for his final semester, which was disappointing, but far better than being killed in the war. Within weeks of these events, Harley would be killed in Vietnam, the very war Dan was trying desperately to avoid. Because of the Vietnam War, Harley was gone, and Dan was sitting in my living room.

Dan told me he was preparing to leave for San Francisco, where his family's business, the Wapakoneta Machine Company had a small subsidiary.

He had recently broken off a long-term relationship, the most serious one he had ever been in. So there we were, two wounded souls drawn together by friendship. Neither of us was ready to jump into another serious relationship, so of course we did. Dan set off for California, all his possessions piled in his tiny car, a Triumph TR250. After a few weeks, he wrote me, his letter sweet and eloquent. We began writing each other regularly, expressing feelings that neither of us ever would have had the courage to say in person. I knew I was in love with him. He was working the night shift, running a machine and not meeting many people. They couldn't keep him there for long. His dad was president of the company. It was only a matter of time before they would find something for him to do on the day shift. Once he was in the sunlight, some devious coquette would spot his handsome young face and snatch him up! I was a desperate woman.

When he offered to pay for half my plane fare to fly out for my vacation, I jumped at the chance to go. Still working nights, Dan arranged for the former guitarist from his college band, Dave Martino, and his wife Ellen, to pick me up at the airport. When they dropped me at his tiny studio apartment in Daly City, an unattractive little suburb just south of San Francisco, we laughed at his Spartan accommodations, the shelves fashioned from bricks and boards, the rented sleeper sofa, and the small round table with only three chairs because he didn't think he "would ever have more than two other people over and a fourth rented chair would have been another $5 a month."

The vacation was wonderful, and as it drew to a close, I knew I didn't want to leave Dan or his table and three chairs. Without really discussing it with him, I called the IBM office in San Francisco to see if they had any openings. Not only did they have an opening, I could start in three weeks, just enough time to dispose of my things and drive out! When I told Dan, he was surprised and excited. Not being sure where exactly the relationship stood, and too shy to ask, I instead asked, "Is it all right if I stay with you until I find a place."

Equally inept at relationships, Dan simply replied, "Sure."

That one little word was about to change our lives forever.

10
Love Is
a Salmon Casserole

Telling my parents I was packing my little Toyota Celica and driving across the country to live with Dan was an interesting character study. My mother reacted as she always did when she was worried: with rage.

"You're going to get out there, and he's going to leave you. We'll have to bail you out just like we always do!" she screamed. That was about as close as she could come to expressing concern over my well-being.

"Oh right, Mother. Like you've ever helped me with anything my entire life."

My dad also behaved the way he usually did. He pouted, the method he normally used to manipulate me into doing what he wanted. It had always worked in the past because I always chose to play the victim role, sacrificing what I wanted to please someone else, and then complaining bitterly because I was so put upon. Much to everyone's surprise, including my own, this time it didn't work. I began selling or giving away my things and arranged to ship a few pieces of furniture. I had a real bed and a table with four chairs.

By the time I left, my mother wasn't speaking to me at all, which, by that time, was a welcome relief. My father drove to Columbus to say goodbye. He stood forlornly in my driveway as I left to begin a new life two thousand miles away over which he would have no control.

Dan and I settled into our own form of domestic bliss, with me working at IBM during the day and him still on the night shift in the factory. It was like an extended date every weekend. We explored the city and generally had fun, but being apart as much as we were, nothing forced us to explore our relationship. We only saw each other on weekends, so we never fought. We probably wouldn't have anyway, because neither of us really knew how. If I was angry, I usually just stuffed the feelings until I exploded like a pressure cooker. That never happened with Dan because neither of us ever expressed an opinion. Dan's family was not abusive, but his father, Lucas, was strong and opinionated. A sweet, sensitive young man like Dan was no match for him in the fighting department. Dan learned early on not to engage him in anything controversial.

Dan's mother, Janet, who I had not yet met, was wife/mother/homemaker extraordinaire, so I imagine my total lack of domestic skills must have been shocking to him. Our family rarely even had meals together after we were out of grade school. Mother worked full time and took classes part time at night, and my dad worked at the post office until 8 p.m. We were rarely ever together at mealtimes. Peggy and I still marvel that either of us ever learned to cook at all. We remember Mother's typical response when we asked "what's for dinner?" Invariably she would reply, "If you big girls can't open a can of soup, you can starve to death" or "Eat some Jell-O."

Neither Dan nor I will ever forget an especially vile casserole I prepared that he ate day after day without complaint. Knowing that he had ulcerative colitis, I bought a cookbook called Bland But Grand. I should have known it was a cruel joke. The recipes were certainly bland, but they were also heinous, which, while more accurate, would not have sold as many copies of the book. The salmon casserole, the only recipe I actually prepared from the cookbook, consisted of canned salmon, mushy canned peas, canned mushrooms and some sort of putrid milky sauce to hold it together. There was no seasoning of any type. Not only did it have almost no taste, but it had a strange, slimy texture, weird pink coloring, and it smelled nasty. I tasted it when I made it on Monday, and I immediately knew it would never pass my lips again. There was, after all, nothing wrong with my colon; and even if there had been, it could not possibly have been severe enough to get me to eat salmon casserole again under any circumstances. I would have thrown it out after the first day, but I noticed that it was disappearing. We didn't have a garbage disposal, so apparently, I thought, Dan liked it. He couldn't be feeding it to the cat because we didn't have one. When I finally saw Dan on Saturday and expressed my horror and surprise that he had continued eating that putrid casserole every day, he just smiled and said, "Yeah, it was pretty bad, but I didn't want to hurt your feelings."

I should have known at that moment that he loved me unconditionally, and would forgive me almost anything. It is a quality that has proven invaluable over the years in our relationship, and it is obviously part of our sacred contract.

Fortunately, our friend Ellen Martino and her mother were both excellent cooks, and they took pity on us. They taught me most of what I know about cooking, most importantly that if a recipe calls for a half cup of wine, it isn't necessary to measure the wine. Instead, tip the bottle and pour until whatever is being cooked is the right color. Whatever wine is left is reserved for the cook. That valuable lesson also taught me to never cook with cheap wine.

After a few months, Dan was promoted to Shipping Manager. The title was deceiving because he was, in fact, the entire shipping department for this tiny company. He built the wooden crates to send knives all over the world, and he delivered knives in the greater Bay Area in a little Volkswagen truck. The truck was small, but enough to land him in the Teamsters' Union. Details of the job notwithstanding, the best part was that he was finally working days, and we finally had the opportunity to get to know each other. While he was kind and funny, I found Dan to be aloof, not easy to draw out. It never occurred to me that he was just as insecure in the relationship as I was. I thought it meant he didn't like me. The status of the relationship came to a head when the lease was up on his tiny studio apartment. We both knew we would be moving, but neither of us was certain how the other felt and neither wanted to ask for fear of being rejected. Consequently, we didn't know if we were moving to one apartment or two. I called Ellen one day, frantic.

"It's time to find a new apartment. Dan hasn't told me if he wants to live together or not. I don't know what to do," I sobbed.

"Have you asked him?" Ellen responded calmly.

Her rationality annoyed me. I was in crazymaker crisis mode. I didn't want a simple solution. "I couldn't do that. What if he said he wanted me to find my own place?" I whined.

"Well, then you would know to start looking for an apartment, and maybe even a roommate." Ellen was a no-nonsense business woman, and she wasn't about to listen to any foolishness from me.

Reluctantly, Dan and I sat down to talk about our immediate plans. "So do you want to look for a new apartment together or would you rather get one by yourself?" I asked hesitantly, waiting for the other shoe to drop.

"What do you want to do?"

"I don't know. What do you want to do?" Back and forth we went, both afraid to voice an opinion. We were pathetic.

Finally Dan said softly, "I was kind of hoping we'd stay together."

It wasn't until months later I learned that Dan had also called Ellen and had the same silly conversation she and I had shared. She gave him the same stern advice.

We left dreary Daly City for the beauty of Marin County, north of San Francisco. Our new apartment had a balcony that overlooked Mount Tamalpais, considered a sacred site by the Native Americans. Every morning on our way to work, we crossed the Golden Gate Bridge.

With the change of address, my mother apparently finally realized that I wasn't going to be finding a place of my own. No, I was living in sin! That's when the phone calls in the middle of the night began.

Dan and I were never certain if she realized it was the middle of the night in California, but nonetheless it was incredibly annoying to be jolted from a sound sleep to the whining voice of my mother on the other end of the phone. The conversation was always the same.

"Naaannncy?"

"Yes, Mother."

"I can't believe you're living in sin. I didn't raise you to be a little slut. I can't walk down the streets of Wapakoneta and hold up my head, because you're living in sin. He's never going to marry you, and no decent man will ever want you now."

"Look, Mother. I'm 2,000 miles away from anyone you know. In the first place, it's nobody's business how I choose to live. And even if it were, if you weren't telling everyone you know, no one would even know we were living together. I'm happy. It's nobody's business if I'm living with Dan or not. What 'they' think doesn't bother me. If it bothers you, stop telling 'them'." Then I would hang up and try to go back to sleep.

We finally stopped answering the late-night calls, figuring that we didn't need to hear any more about my mother and her drooping head. We were 2,000 miles away from our families; any other bad news could wait until morning. Eventually she stopped calling.

That was the only contact I had with my mother while I was in California, and I didn't hear much from my dad either except for the occasional card. It was a difficult time for my dad though. In one card he wrote a note that said, "I'm awful sorry if Danny was offended by what I said about you being all alone out there. I didn't mean it that way. I just meant you were out of reach of your family. You can tell him I'm sorry. I'm sending $20. Take Danny out for dinner." For the first time in my life, I was completely out of his control, but more importantly, Dan was a serious threat to unseat him as the center of my universe. He was losing control, and there was nothing he could do about it. I was as happy as I had ever been, and I no longer looked to him for emotional support.

He couldn't have been pleased with what was happening, but I certainly was. I had a great job, a man I loved who treated me well even if he didn't express his feelings as much as I would have liked, and I was finally free from my mother. It didn't occur to me on a conscious level that I was also breaking away from my father.

11
One Hair at a Time

After about six months in our new apartment, I decided that it was time to get married. Still insecure about the relationship, I wanted the security I believed a marriage license would provide. At dinner one night at the dining room table–the one with four chairs–I said, "I think it's time to get married."

Always the romantic, Dad said, "OK."

Now I had done it. I said the "M" word and he said "OK." It was time to plan a wedding.

I had no experience in planning a wedding; I only knew that I didn't want a repeat of what my sister had agreed to experience. Peggy came home from college in the spring believing all the plans were set for her late-June wedding only to discover that Mother had cancelled all of the arrangements. The stress of a wedding was more than my mother could bear, and Peggy had to scramble to move the event to her fiancés tiny church 120 miles away. Mother and Dad arrived late for the ceremony because they were watching cartoons in their hotel room and lost track of the time. When they did arrive, Mother was in a wheelchair because of a back problem and was wearing a black bouffant wig! Just as I didn't believe my mother set out to ruin Peggy's wedding, I had no reason to believe she would intentionally sabotage mine, but in her fragile emotional state I couldn't take the chance. I was living in California. If I came home to find she had cancelled my plans, I would not have been able to pull a wedding together at the last minute the way Peggy had done.

I couldn't risk my mother's interference. The less my parents knew about the plans, the safer I felt.

I always knew that I would never allow anyone but Dave Ullery to officiate at my wedding. After the Tim debacle, when Dave refused to allow the marriage, I felt even more strongly that he was going to screen any future groom candidates. I called him immediately and reserved his church in Worthington. Dan and I flew home over Christmas and met with Dave, who not only counseled us on marriage, but also recommended a site for the reception, a florist, and an organist. We made all of the arrangements before we went back to California, but I didn't give my parents any details of the wedding except the date, and they never asked for any. It was a modest wedding, the best Dan and I could afford, but it came off without a hitch. With no responsibility other than showing up, my parents had a wonderful time, arriving at the appointed hour under their own power and sporting their own hair.

The years in California were, up to that point, the happiest of my life. After my mother's middle-of-the-night phone calls finally stopped, I rarely heard from her. Being with a man who obviously loved me, although I had no idea why, also lessened my father's influence.

Dan and I were young, with no responsibilities or family obligations, but I was a victim, so I couldn't just relax and enjoy life. Two major fears gnawed at me. When, I wondered, would Dan realize what a terrible mistake he had made in marrying me? Would it be a sudden realization or would it be a gradual erosion of the relationship? I knew it was inevitable, I only wondered if the Band-Aid would be ripped away quickly in one swift yank or if it would be a long, agonizing process, one hair at a time.

Dan never showed signs of unhappiness, but he rarely showed any overt signs of emotion. He was a Fischer, from a long line of old stoic German stock. In fact, he seemed to love me just as I was, but I never completely relaxed in the relationship, sure that it would all unravel soon enough.

On the rare occasions when we would disagree, I would withdraw from the relationship emotionally, insulating myself from the breakup that was sure to follow. When it didn't, I would gradually emerge from my shell like a turtle after a spring rain, peaking out to find him still oblivious to my fatal flaws, and grateful that I had dodged the inevitable bullet for one more day. It's hard to imagine what Dan must have felt during those times of emotional hide-and-seek, which lasted to some degree for more than twenty years. The fact that he rarely betrayed his emotions fed my emotional insecurity because I never really knew where I stood with him save for the fact that he was still there day after day, never changing, never wavering. It would not be until years later that I came to realize and appreciate what a rock of stability Dan had always been in our relationship. For years I believed the only thing that kept him with me was his basic conservatism that made him hate change more than his dislike of me. It never occurred to me during all those years that he was still with me because he loved me. He made it difficult to be a victim, but I always found a way.

My second great fear came to pass when we had been in California about two years. Knowing that the longer we stayed in the Bay area, the more difficult it would be to get us back to Ohio, his dad wrote and said it was time to come "home." I was frantic. We always knew there was a possibility that we would be expected to go back to the main office in Wapakoneta, but I refused to believe it would ever happen. I couldn't go back there. I wouldn't go back there. I would never survive. I was the happiest I had ever been in my life, being exposed for the first time to different cultures, different people, and fresh vegetables (the names of which my family, I was certain, had never even heard). Most importantly, I was free from my mother's craziness. I couldn't go back to tiny Wapakoneta with its cookie-cutter mentality. I didn't fit the mold, and I didn't want to be back in the direct sphere of influence of my family.

"Why do we have to go back? Why can't we just stay here and continue doing what we're doing?" I asked desperately.

"There's no future for me with the company out here. It will be years before I get beyond the Shipping Department."

"Well, why can't you just look for a job out here? You don't have to stay with the family company. You can do something else. I can't go back there."

"Leave the company!!" he shouted. "I can't leave the company! I've planned my whole life to go into the company. It's the only thing I've ever seriously considered doing, and besides, Dad says this would be a good time to come back."

It was the first of only a handful of times that I have seen Dan angry. I not only didn't understand the obligation, but also the pride he felt toward the company. I couldn't comprehend why he was so adamant about leaving California when we were happy.

My only experience with a family business was negative. My father's plumbing and heating business went bankrupt in the early '50s. My experience certainly wasn't like being a part of a successful manufacturing company, which Dan's grandfather had founded in 1891, and which had been run by the family continuously since that time. More importantly, I had no concept of what "Dad says" meant to Dan.

Lucas Fischer was a force to be reckoned with. He was a no-nonsense World War II veteran who spent a large portion of the war engaged in hand-to-hand combat with the Japanese in New Guinea. It was this experience that forged his character and taught him that, above all else, a man was bound by duty. A staunch conservative Republican, Dan often jokingly referred to his dad's political stance as "just to the right of Attila the Hun."

Lucas was well-respected among the rank and file of the company; long-time employees have wonderful Lucas stories. Although he normally had a keen sense of humor, Lucas was in a foul mood on one particular day when he ventured out into the plant to check on the delivery date of an order that was already late. He asked when the order would be shipped. Not picking up on Lucas' dark mood, the plant superintendent picked up a dart and threw it at the wall calendar. Without saying a word, Lucas pulled the dart out of the calendar, moved it up three weeks, and stormed out of the office.

I don't know how Lucas would have responded to direct defiance from one of his children, because no one had ever attempted it, the other three opting instead to move away from Wapakoneta and the family business as quickly as possible. Dan was not about to be the first to force a confrontation, especially when his dream had always been to join the company.

Lucas was opinionated and strong, but in the years I knew him, I can't think of a single incident in which he tried to impose his will on one of his children, save telling Dan it was time to come home. Even then I'm not certain how adamant he was about us returning to Ohio at that particular time. It may have been nothing more than a suggestion, but in any case, Dan believed he had received his marching orders directly from God. While I had issues with my mother that made me want to do the opposite of what she wanted, Dan had issues with his father that made it nearly impossible to ever waver from what Lucas suggested. In addition, Lucas had just undergone a laryngectomy because of throat cancer, so Dan undoubtedly felt a strong obligation to return to Wapakoneta to help in whatever way he could. None of that mattered to me. I was the victim, outraged at what was being done "to" me.

We were young and both ill-equipped to discuss our deep-seated issues with our parents. What was apparent was that I was just as determined not to return to Ohio as Dan was to go back. To make matters worse, I had been with IBM for three years during the glory days of Big Blue, with lavish expense accounts and benefits that included generous relocation packages for employees IBM chose to transfer. Wapakoneta Machine Company was a small, conservative manufacturing company that had never relocated an employee before. I expected that virtually all of our expenses would be paid by the company. Dan and his father, on the other hand, viewed coming back to Wapakoneta as an obligation, a matter of family honor, and therefore our responsibility.

I also believed that being with a family-owned business would automatically bestow privilege, including considerable financial reward. That may be true of many family businesses, but not the Wapakoneta Machine Company. In fact, it was quite the contrary. Lucas made it a point not to distinguish the family members from other employees. The only special privilege was that Dan was held to a higher standard of conduct. There would be no lavish salary package; Dan would receive just slightly more than he was receiving working in the Shipping Department at tiny Cal Saw. Granted the cost of living was less in Wapakoneta than San Francisco, but Dan would only receive five days of vacation a year for the first five years of employment, so the prospects, at least from my human victim perspective, were bleak.

Insecure and totally self-absorbed, I was counting on us not needing any income from me to live well. The only way I could even conceive of living in Wapakoneta was as a social butterfly, playing bridge and lunching with my friends at "the club" or as a radical political activist, whichever I chose. That was not going to be the case.

In full victim mode by this time, I was becoming more frantic, almost crazed at the prospect of moving back to Ohio. It appeared that we would not have the financial freedom to travel at will, to escape what I felt was our exile to the middle of nowhere. I began throwing tantrums, which were totally out of character for me. In response, Dan withdrew. I learned later that withdrawing had always been his response to dealing with his powerful father. He did however talk to Lucas, who agreed to have the company pick up most of our moving expenses. Dan did not attempt to negotiate a better compensation or benefit package because he felt it would be inappropriate. What his father was offering was in line with what other employees were receiving, and that was what Dan would receive also.

As Dan withdrew in response to my ranting, my abandonment issues also became more acute. I felt that Dan was not taking my feelings into account and that he was putting his father ahead of our relationship. He was being torn apart by his desire to please us both, but working in the family business was his dream. This was a powerful drama we had chosen.

Just weeks before we were scheduled to move, I made one last desperate plea, playing the only card I felt I had left.

"Look, Dan, I really love you, and I want to spend the rest of my life with you, but I just can't go back there. I'm not moving back. Are you still going to go?"

We were both in tears, but without hesitation, he replied, "Yes."

I had forced him to choose between me and his dream, and he chose his dream. I felt betrayed, marginalized. Mostly though, I felt angry. I would not soon either forgive or forget. I was not giving any consideration to what Dan wanted or why. I only knew I had an overwhelming, irrational fear about moving back to Ohio. It overshadowed everything else. "Terrible" Tim was short-lived, only about a year; not since I killed Harley had I found such a grand opportunity to play the victim.

12
But It's February, and I'm Suicidal

As moving day approached, I reluctantly agreed to go with him. Dan thought the crisis was over, that everything would be smooth sailing. He couldn't have been more wrong. I agreed to go with him, but I was angry in a way I had never experienced before. It was deep-seated and bitter, always just below the surface, ready to explode. I did everything I could to make sure this anger was not wasted.

IBM offered me an outside sales position in the Lima office. It was a great opportunity for a young woman. It was lucrative, paying more than Dan was making at his father's company, a fact that I threw in his face at every opportunity. I was also IBM's first woman sales representative in conservative little Lima, Ohio. It was 1974, and it was a big deal. In addition to the normal pressures of a high-stress sales job, I also had to contend with the hostile male sales representatives who resented my treading on their sacred domain, as well as almost daily sexual propositions and lewd comments from male customers. I hated my job and I hated Dan. It was a wonderful opportunity to be a victim, however.

We found a nondescript half-double in Lima, which I felt would be more palatable than actually living in Wapakoneta. Besides, I thought, if one of us was going to have a thirty minute commute to work, it should be Dan since he was the one who forced us to move to Ohio. Instead of overlooking Mount Tamalpais, our new place looked out over a farm field, which frequently reeked of manure.

I hated everything about my life. There was no culture, no

restaurants that offered anything other than grease, meat and pota-
toes, or Italian cuisine. The groceries were the worst. Fruits were
limited to apples, oranges, and bananas; the only vegetables they had
were those that could be thrown in a pot with a slab of red meat and
called pot roast. They had never heard of avocadoes or fresh spinach
or any of the other new foods I had come to enjoy. Although they
tried, the grocers were no help. When I desperately asked one if he
had sweet and sour sauce, he replied, "I don't know what that is, but
we have some salad dressing that's kind of tangy." The fact that other
people seemed perfectly happy with their lives only indicated to me
that they just didn't realize how miserable they were.

Any negative, real or imagined, I embraced. I made no attempt
to adjust to my new life. Relishing my victim role, I cried literally
every day for a year.

Of course, there was nothing Dan could do right, no matter how
hard he tried. If I was going to be miserable, which I was determined
to be, then by God he was going to be miserable too–more miserable
if I had my way. It was his fault, and he was going to pay.

The more verbally abusive I became, the more he withdrew, and
the more angry and bitter I became. I was becoming my mother. We
were in a freefall and my only "friend" became my father. He would
stop by almost daily to fix something or just visit. He delighted in
making fun of Dan's inability to repair or assemble anything. Neither
of us took into account that while Dan was growing up, his father
was busy running a company. If anything went wrong at their house,
his mother called someone to repair it. Dan never had anyone to
show him how to do anything around the house, and instead of
taking him under his wing, my father made fun of him. One of my
agreements with my father involved him manipulating my relationships with other people so that it would be the two of us against the
rest of the world, and we could be victims together.

That situation didn't improve when we purchased our first
home in Wapakoneta, about a year after we returned to Ohio. My
dad was able to drop in anytime he wasn't working, where he accom-
plished a two-fold mission: keep me in his grasp by undermining my
relationship with Dan, and ensuring that my mother and I never
developed a relationship at all. He continued his assault on Dan, not
in his presence, but when we were alone he would include little

barbs about Dan in the conversation, always ending with, "But I couldn't love him any more if he were my own son."

His second line of attack was my mother. When he came over, he never missed an opportunity to tell me how miserable he was with her and how she abused him. I used to beg my dad to leave her and move in with Dan and me, never bothering, of course, to ask Dan how he felt. It wouldn't have mattered, because I still harbored so much anger and resentment toward Dan that I was looking for an excuse to ask him to leave. He never would have tried to make me choose between him and my father. My father would have won hands down.

At the same time, my mother and I were barely speaking, usually because my dad told each of us nasty things the other had supposedly said. Mother and I were both victims and both insecure, so we didn't realize the game he played with us until years after he passed over. We didn't understand that we agreed to participate or how well he played his role.

At about this time, Dan was promoted to an outside sales position which, with commissions, nearly tripled his income. It also meant he was on the road, away from home, every week. He liked the job, but hated that he had to leave every Monday morning and not return until Friday. His travel schedule made it even more difficult to maintain a relationship. Dan was gone and my father was there, just the way we wanted it.

The additional income meant I could quit my lucrative but stressful job with IBM. I immersed myself in life in Wapakoneta, joining service clubs such as Junior Service League, learning to play bridge and tennis, and all the other things that go along with suburban life. I was beginning to make new friends, and when Joerdie's husband finished school, they moved to Lima, only 15 miles away. The added income also gave me a temporary ego boost, and slightly elevated Dan's worth in my judgment, because I was finally going to be able to afford the type of lifestyle that I believed would buy me happiness. For the first time since my forced relocation to Ohio, I began to feel a certain degree of contentment. At least I was finally attempting to adjust and forge a new life in Wapakoneta. Of course, I was basing my life on external factors such as material wealth and social status, so my happiness was short-lived. Besides, I wasn't ready to choose not to be a victim.

With Dan gone the entire work week, it wasn't long before I was lonely and bored. I needed more substance and challenge in my life. To fill my time, I took a job with the County Prosecutor's office, where one of my duties involved interviewing and counseling people who had agreed to experience rape and incest. In a county the size of Auglaize, where Wapakoneta was by far the largest town, at 10,000 people, I didn't expect to encounter many such volunteers, but we had three in a three-month period. Without any training, I was surprisingly at ease talking with these young women and children about their experiences. At the time I didn't know that I could identify so readily with them because I too had chosen to experience similar circumstances in this earthwalk. When one little girl described to me what her stepfather had done, I knew exactly what she was talking about, and understood why she felt powerless to stop him. While I was effective in offering support to other people, the images, so close to the ones I held inside, were taking a terrible toll on me. I fondly refer to this as my "crazy period," a time of extreme emotional instability as I struggled for answers, not realizing that I didn't yet know the questions. I suspect, however, that from a human standpoint, this was just one of many crazy periods I chose to experience.

Dan was still traveling Monday through Friday, and I was coming into contact with mostly men in my job. I would like to say that it was because I was young, lonely, and vulnerable that I became involved with a charismatic married man. While all of that is true, by now I know that it was merely our sacred contract.

With Dan gone, I had the freedom to see my lover on almost a daily basis, and it wasn't long before the affair went from casual fling to intense relationship. I was in way over my head. I began attending a fundamentalist Christian church with a friend and quickly embraced its radical, conservative view. My self-esteem already low, and in the throes of a torrid affair, I had no trouble accepting the idea that I was a hopeless sinner unworthy of God's love. I was a victim, and this fit my needs perfectly. While I embraced this new doctrine, which called for repentance and denouncing my sins, I didn't stop seeing my married lover or make any move to end or heal my faltering marriage. I was sinking fast and trying my best to drag everyone I loved down with me.

I began seeing a psychologist in Lima who was recommended by a good friend. Almost immediately he asked me if I had been sexually abused. I dismissed the question as ridiculous. The psychologist never broached the subject again, but in retrospect I can see now that he treated me for the individual symptoms of abuse, probably the best he could do under the circumstances. Obviously, with the symptoms I exhibited, he suspected incest. I would later discover that my behavior was textbook for a person who has chosen to experience sexual abuse.

I saw the doctor at least twice a week because I was right on the edge. My behavior, especially at work, was becoming more and more erratic. I was belligerent, having almost daily battles with my co-workers over virtually nothing. The psychologist gave me books on self-esteem and empowerment, which did help to a small degree. We worked on releasing anger by beating on pillows. Being a victim, I had plenty of anger, enough to share with almost anyone.

Dan knew something was terribly wrong, but had no idea what it might be. He attributed much of my behavior to the stress of my job and the fact that he was gone all of the time. I refused to consider quitting my job, so Dan talked to his father, who agreed that he would become Assistant Sales Manager, which meant he would only travel a few days a month rather than every week. While Dan believed his presence would improve my situation, it only hastened my breakdown. No longer able to see my lover on a regular basis, my depression deepened and the downward spiral I chose to be on accelerated to break-neck speed.

I was married to a wonderful man but could barely stand to be in the same room with him; I was having an affair with a married man; I was in a stressful job, interviewing people who agreed to abusive experiences that mirrored the ones I also chose; and I was a speaking-in-tongues born-again Christian, which added a huge helping of guilt to round out the equation. It was a dream situation for a professional victim. I reached my breaking point. One day I went to work, had a terrible fight with a co-worker over something trivial, and walked out. I went home and took a bottle of pills, my weapon of choice in the suicide game.

This was the time I tried the prescription allergy medicine and just had really dry nasal passages for an entire week, but it was still enough to land me in the psychiatric ward of the hospital for a month. Being a psychologist rather than a psychiatrist, my regular therapist was not permitted to treat me during my hospital stay, so I had daily sessions with one of the staff psychiatrists, a young Asian man with a limited command of the English language. I was already depressed, my life in turmoil, and I was only going to be seeing this man for the duration of my hospital stay. I had neither the energy nor the desire to go into the sordid details of my personal life, and at that point I'm not certain I wanted to get better. Every morning it was the same routine.

"How you do now, Nancy?" he would ask, his young face eager with the anticipation of a major breakthrough in my treatment that day.

Every day my response was the same. "Fine," I would answer flatly.

"Good, good," he would reply, his face clearly showing the disappointment of realizing that I would not provide the material for his first medical journal article.

Because I chose not to participate, the actual treatment was not dramatic, but the hospital stay was a godsend, a time for solitude and reflection, two things sorely lacking in my life. While I didn't significantly change my personal circumstances, I did make the decision to quit my job. The stress of dealing with other people who had chosen to experience abuse was removed, but so was the opportunity to see my lover, who I had met through my job.

After a month, the hospital released me although I was not substantially better than the day I arrived except for my new appreciation for post-nasal drip. My young doctor came in to dismiss me. Knowing that this would be his final opportunity to make a profound and lasting contribution to my recovery, he gave it his best shot.

"You go home now," he said in his halting English. "In the spring when the sun shine, you feel much better!" Then he smiled as proudly as if he had discovered the cure for cancer.

"Thank you, doctor. I'm sure I will," I said. It was February; the way I felt at that point, by spring I could be dead. But there was no sense in bursting his bubble. He had found what he believed was a profound pearl with which to leave me. I wasn't going to be the one to tell him otherwise.

13
Unconditional Love

Home again and unemployed, I had plenty of time to be really miserable, and no one was going to stop me. In retrospect, I don't know how Dan held our lives together during that time. I certainly didn't do anything to help. Obviously it was part of our agreement together. I alternated between sobbing uncontrollably and sullen silence when he was home. When he wasn't home, I got stoned and spent hours listening to depressing music, lying on the floor, knees drawn up into the fetal position, rocking, sometimes violently, back and forth.

Despite his best efforts to help me, Dan was hampered by the fact that he didn't know about the married lover and neither of us knew that I had chosen to experience sexual abuse this earthwalk. He was at a loss to understand why I was depressed. He kept pleading with me. "I want to help you with your problem. Just tell me what to do."

The fact that he kept referring to it as "my problem" infuriated me. It was our problem, perhaps only his, and I was the helpless victim of his heinous acts. If only he hadn't been traveling so much, if only he hadn't forced me to move to Ohio. I was not willing to take any responsibility for my own life; I blamed him.

As I continued to see my regular psychologist several times a week, the obvious signs of depression were beginning to wane slightly. After months, he finally convinced me that I would have to choose between Dan and my married lover. The choice was Dan or no Dan. Since the suicide attempt, Dan was always home at night, afraid to leave me alone, and so there was no opportunity for me to see my lover. Besides, even though it had been an intense relationship, neither of us had given serious consideration to leaving our spouses. It was an affair, and it was time to end it, although I knew it was already over. My therapist convinced me that I had to tell Dan. He had stuck by me all those months, not knowing what was wrong, and now I had to give him the option of leaving or trying to salvage the relationship.

Telling Dan was by far the most difficult thing I have ever done in my life. I knew how much it was going to hurt him, yet I had to do it. If we were going to salvage the relationship, we had to begin with the truth. The direct approach seemed the best, so I simply said to him, "I've been having an affair for over a year. I'm going to end it now. What do you want to do about our relationship?"

With tears welling up in his eyes, Dan replied, "I want to work it out."

I knew before I asked the question that this is what he would say. He had signed on for the long haul, for better or worse, and it didn't get much worse than this. It wasn't until that moment though that I realized what incredible strength Dan possessed. We had been through hell together on this journey we chose. Even so, he was committed to continuing the relationship. He loved me unconditionally.

The road ahead was going to be almost as rough as the one we had just covered, but now we would both be working toward the same goal. We were in the battle together, but we didn't know that I had chosen to experience sexual abuse and was manifesting much of the behavior that accompanies that particular choice. We could work to repair the damage my affair had caused in our relationship and the resentment I felt toward him for moving back to Ohio, but without knowing about our various sacred contracts, it would be difficult to eliminate their effects.

The therapy was grueling since neither Dan nor I had a clue how to communicate with each other. In the six years we had been together, we rarely fought. We always avoided confrontation.

My parents' contract included fighting incessantly, cursing and screaming horrible things at each other while they worked on whatever lessons they were trying to learn. I can barely remember a conversation the two of them had that didn't eventually deteriorate into screaming. I was determined that I was never going to have that kind of relationship with anyone, even if it meant always stuffing my feelings. Consequently I generally avoided confrontation by not voicing an opinion. It had the added benefit of always allowing me to be a victim. I stuffed a lot of anger and frustration and resentment over all those little, seemingly unimportant things, like leaving the lid off the toothpaste or removing his socks and underwear in one motion so that they were still attached to each other on the bedroom floor. All the little annoyances that couples work out in the first months together we had been harboring for six years.

Dan's approach was similar, but for different reasons. While Dan came from a loving family, his father was tired and frustrated from years of running the company. Rather than take his frustration out on his employees, he would instead come home, have a couple of martinis with Dan's mother, and by the time they sat down to dinner together, he became a screaming tyrant. While there was never a safe time to approach my mother, Dan knew that with his father he could only approach him first thing in the morning or in the time between his arrival home from work and before he finished the first martini. After that, he and his younger brother knew to just sit and be quiet. Lucas was not angry with the family, but the children learned not to get caught in the crossfire by saying the wrong thing when Lucas was on the rampage. Consequently, Dan also stuffed a lot of his emotions and frustrations in order to maintain a calm home front. His body responded by manifesting ulcerative colitis, which is caused, as Dr. Welby succinctly put it, "not by what he was eating, but by what was eating him." Dan's colitis was at its worst during the early years of our marriage.

In therapy, we had to begin to really talk to each other. Since both of us were writers, the therapist had us each make written lists of things that annoyed us about the other and then read them aloud during our therapy sessions. When it came time to share our lists with each other, I panicked, telling the therapist that I couldn't possibly share those things with Dan because I didn't want to hurt his feelings, as though the preceding months' events hadn't already gotten his attention. In reality it was the fear that if I voiced my opinion and shared my needs, I would be rejected. On the other hand, if Dan changed his behavior and the relationship improved, I could no longer be a victim, but I didn't recognize that yet.

The therapist gave me more books to read, with titles like *Stand Up! Speak Out! Talk Back!* and *Your Perfect Right.* They helped, but only marginally. I would have a strong dose of assertiveness immediately after reading the book, but it would quickly fade and I would slip back into victim mode. My emotions were numb from the years of abuse I had chosen to experience, so, in many cases, I truly didn't know how I felt. The therapy did help us to understand that we didn't know how to communicate, but it was not until the flashbacks began 20 years later that I learned about Classroom Earth and the choices we make.

14
Everything Changed

In our family, where we all chose to be victims, the closest thing to nurturing any of us ever received was when we were sick. Consequently, all of us were as seriously ill as we could be, as often as possible. Having major surgery was a bonus because recovery time was longer and our moment in the nurturing spotlight was extended. My father was king of the phantom illness, often going from doctor to doctor until he would find one who would confirm some dire disease, or at least admit him to the hospital for diagnostic tests. His stomach looked like the intersection of a main rail line, with criss crossing scars from various surgeries. He even had a veterinarian friend whom he would occasionally consult with his vague and mysterious symptoms.

When he became ill on New Years Day in 1982, I knew it was different, somehow more serious. I could see genuine fear in my father's face.

I rushed him to the hospital in Lima, where they immediately admitted him; he was, by this time, doubled over from excruciating pain. He had been suffering from a mild bout of phlebitis for several weeks, and now it seemed a blood clot had broken off from his leg and lodged in his lung. My dad was in serious trouble. The doctors began a regime of blood thinning drugs to dissolve the clot, but just when they expected him to be getting better, he took a sudden and dramatic turn for the worse. Drifting in and out of consciousness, my father hovered near death for nearly six weeks. His doctors were baffled. Finally his veterinarian friend diagnosed that he had developed Addison's dis-ease, a deterioration of the adrenal gland. Apparently the drug necessary to dissolve the blood clot and save his life had destroyed his adrenal gland.

In her book *You Can Heal Your Life*, renowned author, Louise Hay discusses how our mental patterns and emotions create the dis-eases our physical bodies manifest. As a follower of Hay's work, I have chosen to spell dis-ease with a hyphen, to signify that the root cause of illness is almost always emotion based. We are not at ease with our emotions.

After much research, Hay has documented the specific emotional causes of various dis-eases. According to her research, Addison's Dis-ease is caused by severe emotional malnutrition and anger at the self, defeatism, and a feeling of no longer caring for the self. This was certainly an appropriate dis-ease for a soul that has agreed to experience being a pedophile.

The news for my father was not good, but at least we knew what we were dealing with. There was no cure but with the aid of drugs, in this case huge quantities of the steroid Prednisone, the average life expectancy was four years. He would have to make severe lifestyle changes—including retiring from his job as a disgruntled postal worker. He had to eliminate as much stress as possible from his life because his body no longer produced adrenaline, the "fight or flight" substance that the adrenal gland normally secretes for times of stress. In his case, sudden shock or trauma could result in death.

My father was scheduled to be released from the hospital in a few days. Meanwhile, Dan and I were experiencing a major change of our own.

Early one morning, the director of the county Welfare Department called me. He and his co-worker wanted to come by at 9 a.m. for a visit and I needed to have my husband come home from work to meet with them. Since I normally didn't have occasion to deal with the Welfare Department, I had no idea why they were coming to see us, but I did as they asked and called Dan to come home.

The Director and his assistant got right to the point. Two years before, because of infertility, we had registered with the Welfare Department to adopt a child. We hadn't heard from them since, and had given it very little thought. Now the Director's words were spinning wildly in my head. I managed to focus enough to hear him say, "We have a little girl, twenty-two days old, and if you are interested we'll bring her at two o'clock."

Were we interested? Of course we were interested! Dan and I had been living together for ten years, married nine of them. We had been trying to have a child for years. We had undergone almost every infertility treatment available at the time and had experienced one miscarriage.

So that was it then. In five hours, we were going to be parents. We were not prepared in any way, other than desperately wanting a child. The last child I had taken care of was Dave and Beth Ullery's son Steve who was by that time a sophomore in college. I remained outwardly calm, assuring Dan that everything was under control. I must have been convincing, because he went back to work, leaving the situation in what he mistakenly believed were my capable hands.

I did what I always do in a panic situation: I called Joerdie.

"We're getting a baby; they're bringing her at two," I sputtered, nearly hyperventilating. "What do I need? What should I do?"

As calmly as she could in such an extraordinarily exciting time, Joerdie explained that I would need diapers and bottles and formula, and of course some sacs for the baby to wear.

"No problem," I said. "I just went to the grocery and I have plenty of sacks."

Finally grasping the gravity of the situation, Joerdie replied with only a hint of anxiety in her voice, "I'll go with you."

So off we went to every store in Lima that might conceivably sell baby items and bought more clothes, blankets, toys, and you-name-it than any five children could use. We bought a beautiful hand-knit pink outfit with matching hat and booties that we dropped off at the Welfare Department for our new daughter to wear when she met us for the first time. On our way home, we stopped at the school where my mother was teaching to tell her she was about to become a grandmother for the fourth time. She appeared pleased, but didn't let her guard down enough to show any real excitement in my presence.

We live in a small town where word travels fast. By one o'clock, an hour before our baby was to arrive, we had everything we needed for instant parenthood. One friend showed up with a portable crib for us to use, another with a changing table, others with diapers and clothing. It was amazing. The child would want for nothing.

Dan arrived home just before our daughter. The doorbell rang, and there stood the Director and his assistant holding what appeared to be an immense bundle of pink blankets. As the assistant handed her to me, she smiled and said simply, "Here's your daughter." I'm sure that holding their new child for the first time is a memory no parent will ever forget. Because we had almost no time to grasp the idea, the simple act of being handed our child is one of the most vivid and precious memories of my life.

It was a cold February day, and I carefully peeled away each blanket layer until I finally uncovered the perfect little pink face beneath. She was incredibly beautiful and looked adorable wearing the little pink outfit Joerdie and I had chosen for her.

We spent the rest of the afternoon holding her and smiling in disbelief. We really were parents. Joerdie stayed with us to take pictures of the event and to show me the bare necessities of motherhood. She did her best to teach me the rudimentary skills that I would need to take care of an infant. The only instructions we received with the baby were written on a single sheet of paper: "Powder and feed on demand." When I wondered aloud how I would know when she was demanding to be powdered, Joerdie patiently explained that they were two separate instructions.

By evening, a line of people had formed at our front door, all coming to see the baby and all bearing gifts. We hadn't even called people to tell them; word just spread through the town. You would have thought they were coming to see the Christ child, and for us she was just as precious. One neighbor who had not heard the news saw the line of cars in our driveway and assumed my father had passed over. When she stopped by to make a condolence call, she was thrilled to learn her mistake.

As the people arrived, each said, "Oh! She's beautiful! What's her name?" Name? We had barely begun to comprehend that we had a baby; we hadn't even discussed a name. We had to think fast. Joerdie and Eric were our dearest friends, but two Joerdie Fischers even if the Fischer/Fisher was spelled differently was too much. Instead we chose Erica in honor of her godfather, Eric. For her middle name we chose Lynn, because it seemed to fit, and didn't realize until later that her initials were E.L.F. We fell into bed exhausted, expecting to take turns sleeping in short stints while the other got up to care for the baby. Much to our surprise and delight we discovered that at twenty-two days old, our precious elf was already sleeping through the night. We knew at that moment that she was a gift directly from God/Goddess. Who else would know to give two loving but otherwise inept parents such a perfect child?

The next day, my dad was released from the hospital. He was frail and weak, down to 135 pounds from his six-week ordeal in the hospital. He didn't have the strength to do much, but he was able to drive to my house for breakfast every day with me and the little girl he obviously adored. And so the ritual began from the time Erica was born until the day he went to the hospital for the last time almost eleven years later; if Grandpa was in town, he was at our house for breakfast with the little girl he dubbed his "Petey guy." (His last name was Peterson and many people called him Pete, thus the nickname for Erica.) The moment Erica was old enough to speak she informed him, "No, Grandpa, I'm a girl, not a guy." To him she became simply Petey.

The two were great buddies, almost inseparable. He was always our first choice as a babysitter, and he was eager to spend any time he could with her. When I went back to work, Erica was about two. Grandpa would make certain that after our breakfast together, she was bathed and dressed before he drove her to the sitter's and, as she got older, to school. They played together for hours; there was seemingly nothing too ridiculous for him to do for her. When at two Erica received her first play kitchen he would obediently follow her instructions to "Sit. Eat" on the tiny plastic chairs that were part of the set. He would sit and eat whatever mushy treat she provided until they moved to the next game. Every open house, every school event, anything involving Erica, he was there. Things he never would have attended for his own children, he gladly sat through for her.

When her goldfish died and I was about to flush him away to fish heaven, she became hysterical. I had told her about all the cat funerals we had as children and how we would always sing "Rock of Ages" from an old hymnal. She was determined her fish would have just as grand a send-off. I had to go to work and couldn't stay for the main event, so Grandpa had to handle it. As every neighbor and I left for work that day, we could hear Grandpa and Petey bellowing out "Rock of Ages" as they buried the goldfish in the backyard.

Even on the last day he was home, hemorrhaging from the effects of the Prednisone, he managed to drive her to school one last time. Then he went home and called the Rescue Squad to take him to the hospital. He nearly bled to death before they reached the hospital, but nothing would have prevented him from driving his Petey to school. She was the greatest joy of his earthwalk.

We don't know what Erica's sacred contract was with her grandfather, but it doesn't matter. We understand that nothing could occur to which she did not agree.

15
A Pyrrhic Victory

In the fall of 1992, it became obvious to everyone around him that my father's health was deteriorating rapidly. He had been in and out of the hospital with rectal bleeding several times in the weeks before his final stay. Each time the doctors managed to stop the bleeding and stabilize his condition, but it was apparent he was getting worse. Because of his medication, his organs were becoming thin and fragile, like tissue paper. At the time, the average life expectancy of someone with Addison's Dis-ease was four years, and he had lived with it for nearly eleven years. We all knew he was living on borrowed time. He felt certain that if he began hemorrhaging again the doctors would be forced to remove his colon. He told me many times that he feared living with a colostomy bag far more than he feared death.

On that last morning, he came for breakfast as usual, but he was acting strange, going to the bathroom often and generally appearing agitated. I asked him if he was bleeding again; he just nodded. When Erica appeared, dressed and ready for school, he got up from his chair and walked slowly toward the door. I said, "Daddy, if you're too sick, I can take her to school. In fact, why don't I call the Rescue Squad and get you to the hospital?"

"No, I'm fine," he protested. "After I drop her off, I'll go home and call the doctor and see what he wants to do."

I kissed him goodbye, but as I moved forward to hug him he put up his arm and held me back, afraid that any jarring to his body would increase the bleeding.

As I drove to my office, twenty miles away, I knew that my dad was not all right, that this time was far more serious than ever before. Filled with dread, afraid that he was going to die, I did not know how I would survive without him. In our sacred contract, he and I both chose to be victims, but it was always the two of us against the rest of the world.

Deciding to stop in at my office and then head home to check on Dad, I listened to my voice-mail messages and heard my mother. Because she had never before called me at work, I knew it couldn't be good news.

Her message was frantic. "Leo had a massive hemorrhage. He's on his way to the hospital. I'm on my way now."

I left work immediately, so distraught that I drove ten miles south on Interstate 75 instead of north before I noticed I was going the wrong direction.

After he dropped Erica off at school, my dad headed home. He made it as far as his back steps. He managed to get inside and call for an ambulance. While he waited for them to arrive, he went back outside and tried unsuccessfully to wash the blood off the steps and sidewalk so that my mother and I would not have to find it.

On the way to the hospital, my dad continued to hemorrhage, and nearly bled to death. His doctor was waiting in the emergency room when the ambulance arrived. He began working on my dad immediately. By the time I arrived, my mother was already there. She was hysterical, screaming, "He's going to die! He's going to die!"

Equally frantic, I screamed back at her, "He isn't going to die! He can't die! Just shut up! He isn't going to die!"

His cardiologist and an internist came out to give us an update; it was obvious from their faces that the situation was grim. My dad's heart stopped beating, but they were able to restart it. He was stabilized for the moment, on a respirator, but the blood was now flowing out faster than they could pump it back in with transfusions. Despite the risks, they were going to take him into surgery to stop the bleeding. There was no other choice.

Believing that my father would not survive the surgery, I began screaming and crying hysterically while my mother continued ranting, "He's going to die!" Dan, who had arrived at the hospital, was trying with very limited success to calm us both.

Before they took him to surgery, Mother and I went in to see him and presumably tell him goodbye. He was on a respirator. He couldn't speak, but his eyes were filled with terror. Clearly he didn't want to have the surgery, but he knew it was his only chance. I cried and told him I loved him.

The surgery lasted for hours, and while he was gone, I called Peggy in Lancaster, about 120 miles away. My mother and I always had a volatile relationship, especially when it involved my father. We constantly went out of our way to do the opposite of what the other wanted. Mother did, however, occasionally listen to Peggy. While I learned to be defiant in order to survive the crazy childhood we chose, Peggy became passive. She usually under-reacted to any situation. The result was often that she let me take either the blame or responsibility, whichever was appropriate at the time. Peggy survived by keeping quiet and hoping the bullet would hit me and somehow miss her. It usually did. That was our sacred contract.

It is, of course, difficult to be objective about my own emotional and mental state, but I felt Mother was totally out of control, about to go off the deep end. I suspect I was about to leap with her, but from the opposite side of the pool, of course. I felt I needed Peggy's help to save Daddy's life.

"Daddy's in the hospital. In surgery. He's in really bad shape and Mother is nuts. Can you come up?"

"No. I have to work. I can't come," she replied.

"Look, I need your help. You're the only one she'll listen to. I have a job, too, and a family. I'm here. Can't you please come?" I begged.

"Well, is he going to die?" she asked almost casually. "I'll come up if he's going to die."

At the time Peggy was working for the Board of Elections. It was fall, a few weeks before a major presidential election, a nearly impossible time for her to get away. My father's entire life had been one health crisis after another from which he always miraculously recovered. Peggy no doubt felt that this was just another of those situations, but I was livid. We didn't know about our sacred contract, so once again I felt she was just leaving me with a responsibility that, because of my relationship with my mother, I was ill-equipped to handle.

"Thanks a lot!" I screamed at her. "I don't know if he's going to die, but if he does I'll be sure to call you." I slammed down the receiver.

The doctors emerged from surgery looking exhausted. The news was grim, but not hopeless. My father was alive, although his heart had again stopped in the recovery room. During the surgery, they removed most, but not his entire colon, so he did not have a colostomy bag. When he was out of the recovery room and awake, we would be able to visit him in the coronary intensive care unit. Neither doctor gave us a long-term prognosis for recovery, but the fact that he had survived the surgery was nothing short of a miracle. My father always had a strong will to survive. He had been in tough positions before when we thought he wouldn't make it, and he always pulled through. I was certain that he would make it this time too, primarily because I didn't believe I could face life without him.

By the time Daddy was taken to his cubicle in CICU, Peggy had arrived. Daddy was awake, alert, and obviously in tremendous pain. Even though he had a morphine pump, it wasn't doing the job. He was grimacing and shaking from the pain. He pushed the button on his pump continually, even though it would only distribute medication at designated intervals. Still on the respirator, he wrote notes to us saying he needed more medication. There were tubes coming out of every orifice, as well as his incision; some were to drain blood and another, urine; still others were to pump in blood, medication, and liquid nourishment to keep him alive. With monitors everywhere, he was a sight, but I was nonetheless encouraged that he was both alive and awake, convinced that he would make a full recovery.

My mother was insane, standing directly over my father and screaming to anyone who would listen as though he wasn't present.

"Look at him! Just look at him! He looks terrible! He's more dead than alive! Just look at him. This is terrible!"

With each barrage, my dad became more agitated. His blood pressure shot up and his heart rate increased. The nurses tried to calm her down. They finally asked us all to wait in the lounge "so he could rest."

I called his doctor. "Can you slip my mother some sort of tranquilizer?" I asked. "She's absolutely wild, and she's upsetting my father. She stands directly over him screaming how terrible he looks, and then his blood pressure and heart rate shoot up. Can't you give her something?"

"No, I can't do that. She's not my patient, and besides, I'd have to have her consent. She'd never agree to it."

He decided instead to sedate my father. He would give him a drug that would keep him in a near-comatose state. He would be able to hear us, but not likely to respond, and when he recovered, he would not have any memory of the ordeal. The important thing was that he would remain quiet, not fully aware of Mother's ranting, and it would give his body an opportunity to heal. My father agreed and signed the consent form. By doing so, he placed all future decisions about his care in Mother's hands. He would be virtually unconscious, unable to communicate in any meaningful way. She was his next of kin.

Peggy went back to Lancaster, believing the situation was stable. None of us realized that because of our sacred contract, Mother and I had been rivals for control of my father and his affection all of my life. Now the fight had reached a whole new level, with Mother holding most of the cards.

Both Mother and Daddy had signed living wills months before his condition had deteriorated, stating that neither wanted to be kept alive on machines or by any other extraordinary means. My father was placed on a respirator in the emergency room when his heart stopped; I believed the living will was basically moot. The respirator is an extraordinary measure, but once a person is placed on it, the hospital will not remove it until the patient can either survive without it, or passes over. Since extraordinary means were already in effect, I felt we should do everything possible to give him a fighting chance. Mother, on the other hand, felt that she should honor the living will, but she decided that any treatment at all was extraordinary. We were at an impasse.

While his vital signs were generally acceptable, my father continued to bleed from his rectum. It was not a hemorrhage like he had experienced before, and the doctors wanted to examine him to see if they could determine where the bleeding was coming from. It wasn't an invasive procedure, just an examination, but Mother refused to allow it. She would only allow fluids, nourishment, antibiotics, and blood transfusions, just things that could be administered intravenously or through the myriad of tubes already attached. She specifically forbade anything else. There was nothing I could do, nothing the doctors could do. I felt completely powerless and frustrated, once again a victim. I had always hated the woman, but now I wanted to kill her—I mean really wanted to kill her. I believed she was actually facilitating my beloved father's death, and I had no way to stop her. I was almost certainly just as irrational and out of control as she was by this time, but I felt I was the voice of reason. She was insane. I believed I was the only thing standing between my father and certain death; I had to protect him. I contacted my attorney to try to have her declared incompetent, but gave up on the idea because he felt I didn't have enough evidence. What more evidence could I possibly need, I wondered? She was obviously trying to kill him.

The only thing I could do was try to keep her as calm and reasonable as possible so that she would let the doctors do what they could to help my father. To me that meant I had to stay at the hospital all the time so that she couldn't do anything to hurt him while I was gone, and I had to try to get along with her.

Mother respected Dan. Perhaps he could get her to listen to reason, get her to at least give my father a fighting chance to survive, but Dan had left for California on business. When I realized how serious my dad's condition was, I had begged him not to go, but he insisted he had no choice. There was an important trade show in Los Angeles, and he didn't have anyone else at the time who could represent the company. I couldn't imagine anything in the world more important than protecting my father, and I also needed help with Erica who was being shuffled among friends and babysitters. At that moment I hated Dan for leaving me alone when I really needed him. I had never asked him not to make a trip before, but this time I had begged him to stay and he refused. I knew it would take me a long time to forgive him, and it did. I was in full victim crazymaker mode.

Everything remained stable for the first week. My father didn't get noticeably better, but he didn't get worse either. I felt the longer he hung on, the better his chances of making a recovery. I rarely even checked in at work during that period, but I encouraged

Mother to go to work, go home, and get some rest, anything to get her out of the hospital and away from my dad. It was clearly a competition between us, with my father as the prize. Sometimes I would pretend I was going to work so that she would leave also. Then I would sneak back in to sit with my dad, hold his hand, and talk to him silently.

"Just hang in there," I would say mentally. "You've been through worse than this before. You can get through this too. Just rest and concentrate on getting better. I have a lot of strength and you can have every ounce of it. We'll get through this together. I'll stay here with you as long as it takes. Please get well, Daddy. I need you."

On October 4, two weeks after the surgery, he took a sudden turn for the worse. His heart rate and blood pressure spiked and he developed a high fever. His primary doctor was not on call that weekend; the doctor in charge, not knowing the situation, didn't question my mother's instructions to do nothing.

It was Sunday, and I spent the afternoon with Erica. Dan was still gone, and I had barely seen her since the ordeal with my dad had begun. When I arrived at the hospital after dinner, my mother attacked me.

"Where have you been?" she screamed. "I tried to call you. Where were you? You should have been here."

"I spent the day with Erica. What do you mean, where have I been? Where the hell is your precious Peggy?" I shot back. Peggy had not been back since the day of Dad's surgery. "She's the one who should be here. I've been here every day since his surgery. Why don't you ask her why the hell she hasn't been here instead of tearing into me?"

"Peggy's busy. She's got a family and a job. You should have been here. I told the doctor Leo is going to die, and he agreed with me. He said Leo only has a 10% chance of surviving, so I called the minister. He's on his way."

"I have a family and a job too, you know, so get off my back! Ten percent is ten percent. You have to give him a fighting chance!"

There was no point in arguing with her. We were both beyond the point of listening to reason. Why couldn't she be the one on the brink of death? No one would care, except maybe Peggy. If she were gone, Daddy could move in with us. It would be wonderful.

By the time the minister arrived, my dad's condition had worsened. The three of us began a bizarre bedside vigil, my mother and I no longer speaking to each other at all. We were both just about out of our heads. I held my dad's hand, saying, "I love you, Daddy; just go toward the light."

Mother kept wailing, "Go ahead and go! Go ahead and go!"

The minister was reciting the Twenty-third Psalm. It was pandemonium. I looked at the old wall clock in his cubicle and watched the hand tick off each second. It was 11:55. In five minutes it would be my birthday.

"Please don't die on my birthday, Daddy," I begged silently. "Either go now or wait until later, but please don't die on my birthday."

Immediately he began thrashing wildly in the bed. He had been virtually motionless except for the thrusting of the respirator that was keeping him alive. Something had gotten his attention. It was obvious he was not going anywhere, at least not that night.

I called Dan in California. He said he would catch the first available flight home. There was a pilots' union strike, so there were not many planes flying. It could take days for him to get a flight out. Still angry that he had left when I needed him, I told him I didn't care if he never came home. At the time, I meant it.

Because Dad's condition was so tenuous, the hospital gave us a room to use, reserved for the families of critically ill patients. It was a basic hospital room with two single beds and a private bath, located on the same floor as my dad. Even though I had to share it with my mother, I was grateful to have it. Friends came daily, bringing me clean clothes, so I didn't have to leave the hospital at all, and thus I believed I could protect my father.

The next morning I stood by his bed, holding his hand as the nurse changed the bandages on his incision.

"You really gave us a scare yesterday," I said to him. "I thought we were going to lose you. You're a lot better today, though. Your heart rate is good, and your blood pressure is better. You're going to be just fine. I'm going to stay right here with you. I love you."

With that, the nurse looking on as my witness, my dad opened his eyes and tried to focus. The respirator tube still in his mouth, he looked directly at me and smiled. It was a threshold moment for me.

No matter what the ultimate outcome, I had won once and for all. He had never tried to communicate with my mother. He never tried to communicate with anyone else. In the end, he chose me. He loved me the most.

The euphoria of the bizarre "victory" was short lived. My mother ordered the doctor to stop the blood transfusions. My dad was still bleeding from unknown causes, and the doctors were forbidden to examine him. Too weak to produce enough new blood on his own, without the transfusions my dad would die.

Peggy came up the next Sunday and spent a few hours with Dad. She and I barely spoke. I was angry because while my life was turned upside down, she was seemingly unaffected by Mother and our weird hospital vigil. She had only been there one other time in the three weeks my dad was in the hospital, while I was there every day, yet Mother acted as if Peggy coming to visit was a huge sacrifice. No matter what either of us did, in my mother's eyes Peggy was wonderful and I was nothing. She had never loved me, and she obviously never would. I was also angry because Peggy never tried to defend me, always leaving me to take the blame no matter what the situation. All of that was true, of course, but I didn't understand that it was our sacred contract together. We all played our parts exactly as planned, and I once again chose to be the victim.

I cried on and off the entire afternoon, although I didn't understand why. I was used to stuffing my emotions, but now all that anger and frustration I felt toward my mother and sister was right on the surface. That evening, Peggy gone, and Mother in the lounge with friends, I sat by my father's bed holding his hand.

A sudden calm came over me and I said silently to him, "Daddy, if you want to continue to fight, I'll stay here with you and fight with every fiber of my being for as long as you want. But if you're tired of fighting and want to go home, I understand. I love you more than anything in the world, but I'll be OK. I'll take care of Mother. Do whatever you want to do."

At that moment, the number 7:15 flashed in my mind's eye like the numbers on a digital clock. I looked at the old standard wall clock in his room, the same one that had ticked down the minutes to my birthday just a week before; it read 7:00. I knew he would pass over at 7:15.

Suddenly his blood pressure dropped, and the nurse rushed in, obviously upset.

"Where is your mother?" She asked. "He isn't going to last long."

"I haven't seen her." I lied because I didn't want to share those last precious moments of his earthwalk with her. I sat by my dad's side, holding his hand, while the nurse found my mother and brought her into the room. Mother and I sat quietly on opposite sides of the bed, each holding one of my dad's hands, not speaking to each other. This time there was no wailing, no Twenty-third Psalm. We just sat silently waiting for the end to come. At 7:15, as I knew it would, his heart stopped beating.

I got up and walked around to my mother. Placing my arm awkwardly on her shoulder, I said, "Don't worry, Mother. I'll take care of you." I immediately regretted the promise. I didn't want to take care of her. I hated her. I wanted her dead, not him. He was dead, and she was responsible.

Even though the heart monitor registered a flat line, the respirator continued to thrust my father's lifeless body up and down. In a rage, I yanked at every electrical cord I could find, but the respirator continued pumping air into him. The heart monitor then began flashing a large 7:15, as though I needed any reminder that he was gone. She was there, and he was gone. I couldn't imagine anything worse.

Dan, who had finally made it home two days before, arrived at the hospital with Erica who was expecting to see Grandpa. For weeks I tried as best I could to explain that Grandpa was unconscious and had all sorts of tubes and wires attached to him. He looked pretty scary. He wouldn't be able to talk to her, and might not even know she was there. She didn't care. She wanted to see Grandpa. Now I had to tell her Grandpa was gone. Sobbing hysterically, Erica begged us to let her see him.

By then the nurses had finally disconnected the respirator, removed all the attachments, and propped my father up in bed to facilitate fluid drainage. I slipped behind the curtain of his cubicle to evaluate the situation. Would it be too traumatic for Erica, only ten, or should we let her in to say goodbye as she was begging us to do? He was sitting upright, eyes closed, but his jaw was wide open, nearly touching his chest. Gingerly I tried closing the jaw, but as soon as I removed my hand, it once again gaped open. Even if I held the jaw shut, my dad was bloated and bruised from the weeks of tubes. He looked ghastly, and Dan and I decided that even though it might offer her a degree of closure, the scene was too awful to let Erica see. We didn't want that to be her last memory of Grandpa.

Now it was time to plan a funeral.

16

I Just Got Home Today

The next few days were a flurry of activity, with Mother and me arguing over arrangements for the funeral as though we were both his spouse. We chose the casket and flowers together. She chose the pallbearers, and I picked the music. It was the best compromise we could reach under the circumstances.

The obituary I wrote appeared on the front page of the local paper, along with his picture–the one that six years later sparked the initial memories of the sexual abuse I agreed to experience. The headline read "Public Servant, Leo Peterson, Dies at Age 73." The mayor gave me a plaque in honor of my dad's many years of service to the community.

The line at his visitation wound around the inside of the funeral home, through the lobby, and out into the parking lot, as one might expect for someone as well-known as my father. While I cried almost nonstop when I was at home, at the funeral home it was show time. I greeted visitors, laughing and sharing funny stories about my dad. It was surreal. Joerdie commented to Eric that it wasn't like I was mourning the passing of my father, but rather a long-time lover. She was right, of course, but we didn't know it at the time

The funeral was lovely, with "Rock of Ages" playing softly in the background. No one else understood our last private joke, but I was certain my father was enjoying it.

At my mother's house following the funeral, I realized how much I hated being there without my father. I felt like an intruder, and in a way I suppose I was. Seeing my mother and sister together, I understood that the Fischers were my family now. Mother and I both realized that my vow to take care of her was uttered in the emotion of the moment rather than from any real concern for her well-being, and it was obvious to me that she didn't want me to be a part of her life anymore than I wanted her to be a part of mine.

Mother began disposing of my father's possessions that evening. He had nothing of any monetary value except some tools. I took a couple of pieces of clothing, a broken watch, an old agate ring that I remembered from my childhood, and the tap shoes he made when he surreptitiously took lessons years before. Mother laughed at me and asked if I was going to add them to the shrine I was creating for him. I wanted to cling to any tiny piece of him, and it appeared that she couldn't wait to obliterate any evidence of his existence from the face of the earth.

Every day she filled his little car with his possessions, junk mostly, and took them to the local flea market. I begged her to wait at least a few weeks, when I might be better able to deal with my dad's passing. I would help her sort through his things and decide what to keep. She refused to wait and saved only his car. At the time I felt she was trying to punish me because of my relationship with him. That may or may not be true, but it is more likely that she was coping with her loss in the only way she knew how, by getting on with her life. Whatever her reason, within three weeks every trace of my dad was gone from her house.

Later my mother told me that she found a small stash of pornography, Playboys and the like, and a few paperback sex novels hidden in his workshop. She, of course, had no idea what his real pornography collection had been like. In 1979 my parents moved from the old house on Harrison Street that played such a prominent role in my childhood. When they moved, I helped my dad throw away most of his sexual paraphernalia and books. The pictures that I would later learn he took of me were already gone. I believe he disposed of them when I became old enough to comprehend what they meant. Even then I would not have understood what they really meant because I did not know about our sacred contract.

About three weeks after the funeral, my dad visited my mother in a dream. In the dream she and several of her friends saw my dad walking toward them and, being frightened by a visit from the other side, scattered to hide.

"You might as well come out," he said. "I know you're there. I can see you."

Timidly my mother and her friends came out of their hiding places to face him.

"How much do you remember about the hospital?" she asked.

"Not a thing," he replied, and with that he was gone.

He visited me also, but in a far different and more dramatic way. Choosing full victim mode, I was just barely keeping my head above water, trying to take care of my family, my job, and dealing with intense grief. Erica, a fifth grader at the time, tried to take on as many responsibilities as she could, such as my non-work activities. When she mentioned some function at her school to which I had agreed to bring cookies, I vaguely remembered a message on the answering machine earlier in the day giving instructions. I had promptly erased it.

"Go in and press the play button and see if you can find the message," I told her. "Otherwise, I'll have to call Mrs. Smith."

In an instant she was back, ashen faced and clearly shaken. "I can't find Mrs. Smith's message, Mom, but Grandpa is on there."

I rushed in to investigate. When I pressed the play button, the first message was from my friend Janet Schuler wishing me a happy birthday. This would have been October 5, more than a month earlier, when my father was in a nearly comatose state. The next message was my dad.

"I just got home today," he said. "And I'm hoping to live forever."

There were no other messages following his on the tape. My father passed over on October 11, a full week after my birthday, and in the intervening weeks I had received dozens of other telephone calls, including the one from Mrs. Smith. I replayed the two messages over and over, recording them on my portable cassette recorder. My dad was sending me a message from the other side, letting me know he was fine. The next morning the message light on the answering machine was blinking, and when I pushed it, my dad and Janet were gone, but Mrs. Smith was there, instructing me where and when to bring my cookies.

While I was not familiar with the phenomenon at the time, it is apparently fairly common for loved ones in the spirit world to communicate via the telephone, because they are able to easily manipulate the electrical current.[1]

Although I appreciated my dad's message, I could barely function. It was worse than with Harley's passing because my contract with my father was more intense. When Harley passed over, I only had myself to take care of, and I had his family and my dad to share my grief. This time I had a daughter to take care of, a husband with whom I was angry, as well as a demanding job. Erica was devastated by her grandpa's passing and upset with us because we hadn't allowed her to see him in the hospital. I didn't have the luxury of falling apart. She and I began grief counseling.

During one meeting with the psychologist, I was talking about my mother and how much I resented her. I said, "You know, I really haven't been a very good daughter. I don't call her. I don't see her anymore than absolutely necessary."

She smiled and said, "Of course you are a good daughter. You were a wonderful daughter to your dad."

The psychologist had Erica and me write letters to my father telling him everything we wanted him to know. I didn't read Erica's letter, but mine was a long love letter in which I apologized over and over for not being able to protect him from Mother. I was playing the role of grieving lover, not a daughter.

First and foremost though, I was the victim. I blamed my mother for my dad's death and still could not accept the reality that my father had fulfilled his sacred contract, and left at the time and in the manner he agreed. Nothing the doctors or anyone else could have done would have prevented his passing. I didn't understand any of that. All I knew was that he was dead and she was alive. Nothing I could imagine was more unfair.

After several months in therapy, I still wasn't able to shake the terrible depression I chose to sink into. The counselor suggested that perhaps I should try an antidepressant to help me through. Even though I smoked marijuana regularly when I was younger, I resisted

1. Tom Slemen, a writer who specializes in the supernatural has documented this and other paranormal phenomenon in and around Liverpool, England in "Phone Calls From the Dead" in his book series Haunted Liverpool.

the idea of taking a prescription drug. I reluctantly agreed to meet the psychiatrist, who would evaluate me and determine whether he thought drugs would help me. The doctor, originally from Lebanon, spoke with a thick accent. When I asked him if he felt it was advisable for me to take Prozac he responded, "Oh, better to take." From that point on, we referred to him simply as Dr. Better-to-Take, and I began my six-year love affair with Prozac.

After just a few weeks, the Prozac began to help. I was noticeably less morose. My concentration improved. My sense of humor returned and I developed an inexplicable ability to whistle. While I was still angry with my mother and Dan, at least the open hostility was gone, buried beneath the pink fog the Prozac created. I had chosen to be depressed in varying degrees for most of my life to enhance being a victim, but now I was singing in the shower, eager to face the day. On the surface, Prozac appeared to be a miracle drug, and in many ways I suppose it was. The down side, of course, was that as long as I was taking the Prozac, I didn't feel anything. I was still playing the victim role, but now I was at least cheerful.

17
The
Really
Numb Years

The years from 1992, when my father passed over until my memories began to return in 1998, are significant primarily because I was so numb from the combination of grief, Prozac, marijuana, and my attachment to being a victim that I sleepwalked through some monumental life experiences.

Despite my promise to take care of her, I didn't see much of my mother in the months after my father passed over. While I blamed her for his death, most of the raw anger left within a few months of his passing. Being around her, however, only accentuated his absence, so I chose to avoid the feelings of emptiness by not seeing her.

For her part, Mother was trying desperately to carve out a life for herself. Although my parents shared very few interests, they both loved to dance. Unable to find a dance partner from among the few single men she knew, Mother made a concerted effort to stay in contact by hosting dinner parties for the couples my parents used to dance with, and in return they continued to invite her to their activities. She would accompany the couples to dances, and the men in the group would take turns dancing with her. I'm sure they didn't mind because she was a graceful dancer and fun-loving. Although it wasn't part of her contract with me, Mother had a wonderful sense of humor, and was usually the life of any party. While she appreciated being included with the couples, Mother was lonely.

She turned to personal ads in the area newspapers, but after fifty years of marriage, she was ill-equipped to enter the dating game. She had a few dates with men she met through the ads, but no one with potential for a long-term relationship, or anyone who shared her interest in dancing. One problem may have been that she shaved thirteen years from her age because she didn't want to date "some old man." That probably explains why she generated a lot of initial interest, but no lasting relationships. She looked good for her real age, but was undoubtedly a disappointment to those who were expecting her to be fifty-eight! When one of her friends, a dance instructor, asked if she would help a beginning dancer, a widower from Sidney, Ohio, who had lost his wife at about the same time that my father passed over, she readily agreed. Jim was a nice enough fellow, not nearly as social as my mother, but happy to be keeping company with a funny, attractive woman close to his age. I don't know exactly when Mother and Jim began dating or when they married, because they slipped away to Las Vegas for the wedding. She later explained that she couldn't get married in Wapakoneta because if she applied for a marriage license in our county, the local newspaper would have printed the information, including her age.

Mother and Jim sold their separate houses and bought a house together in Wapakoneta. While they enjoyed each other's company, they had totally different expectations of what marriage should be. Jim's first marriage was traditional; he and his wife didn't have many interests, but none that didn't include the other. My parents, on the other hand, didn't do anything together except dance. Mother belonged to numerous service clubs and bridge groups, while Dad was involved in political and civic organizations. They were both gone almost every night. In fact, they rarely saw each other except when they got together to dance. That suited them fine. Jim, by contrast, expected Mother to stay home with him after they married, and she expected him to entertain himself while she continued her normal activities. Tired of the constant fighting, they sold the house they shared and bought separate, smaller houses of their own, Jim's twenty miles away in Sidney and Mother's in Wapakoneta. They remained married for several more years and saw each other frequently. When the fireworks became too intense, they could retreat to their separate houses.

Mother's marriage to Jim had very little impact on my life. She seemed happy, and I was grateful that I no longer felt obligated to fulfill my ill-conceived promise to take care of her. Jim was never going to be anything more than my mother's husband, and since I didn't have a real relationship with him, I was no longer my mother's rival. Our relationship improved.

Such was not the case with Jim's daughter initially. Apparently always close, Jim and his daughter became even closer after her mother, his wife, became ill and passed over. My mother took an immediate dislike to the woman, criticizing everything she said or did, especially if it involved Jim. She was civil to the daughter, at least in her presence, but Mother reacted to her and her relationship with Jim in much the same way she had done with me and my father although not nearly as fiercely. I suddenly realized that Mother was insanely jealous of anyone she considered her rival, be it Jim's daughter or me. While it was intensely personal to me all those years, it was apparently much less so to my mother. A rival was a rival. Overcoming jealously was a lesson Mother struggled to master this earthwalk. Although she never fully resolved her issues with me, she met with at least limited success with Jim's daughter. By the time Mother passed over, she and the daughter were good friends.

Jim divorced Mother after she suffered a stroke that left her slightly mentally impaired. She refused to stop driving, and Jim didn't want the financial liability if she had a serious accident. It didn't change their relationship; they continued to see each other regularly until she passed over several years later.

I had begun working as the Employment Coordinator at Copeland Corporation, a large manufacturing company in Sidney, Ohio, ten months before my father passed over. The fact that I was even hired by this very conservative company had to be an act of God. On the surface, at least, I appeared to be exactly what they were *not* looking for.

My manager was a bright, funny woman named Bonnie who was conservative even by Copeland standards. While I knew to wear my sensible suit to my initial interview, when I went back a few days later for clerical testing, I was wearing a long, flowing robe of black, turquoise, and purple over a long matching skirt, large dangling earrings, and purple shoes. My previous job was as a cosmetic person in a department store, so I also had flamboyant makeup, heavy on purple and turquoise, and flaming red hair. It was December, and Bonnie was hoping I was on my way to a holiday party. I was not. I might have been eliminated on the spot, Bonnie later told me, if spirit had not continuously whispered in her ear, "Hire the wild one!" I can still hear her gasp the first day the company introduced casual Friday. Everyone else came in their appropriate collared knit polo shirts and khaki pants, while I appeared in a long purple tie-dyed shirt, leggings, and purple loafers. It was the most conservative casual clothing I owned.

At the time I was hired by Copeland, I was smoking marijuana only occasionally, but whether I would have passed a drug screen is unknown, because they never asked me to take one. Verifying degrees and references and administering drug screenings are all standard procedure for Copeland, but they were the responsibility of the Employment Coordinator, the position for which I was applying. The normally detail-oriented Bonnie, over-worked and with no assistant, simply overlooked it. Had she checked, wild dress and makeup notwithstanding, I might not have been hired.

For whatever reason, the Universe wanted me to have this job. Bonnie and I worked remarkably well together, in part because my laid-back style balanced her conservatism. Although my appearance didn't fit the normal corporate image, I was competent and efficient and got along well with people. She began transferring most of the recruiting duties to me, allowing her to concentrate on other areas of her job.

When Bonnie was promoted to a position in another department, a wonderful young man named Darrel took over her higher-level managerial duties such as employee relations and reviews. This was a logical step because he was already responsible for those functions at all of Copeland's outlying plants. The recruiting portion of Bonnie's job became available, and although it was not part of my actual job description, it was precisely what I was already doing. I received the promotion.

The transition went well, and I settled into the new position. Darrel and I also worked well together. With his blessing, I explored new recruiting sources and began hiring significantly more minorities and women for technician and clerical positions. Both were areas where Copeland previously had difficulty meeting the goals suggested by the Equal Employment Opportunity Commission. Now we were meeting, and in many cases even exceeding the commission's recommendations.

About eighteen months into my new job, my dear friend Ellen Martino, in California, had a recurrence of the malignant melanoma she had agreed to experience. What began as a small mole on her back had metastasized to the brain. It was inoperable.

Dan and I remained close to Dave and Ellen since the early '70s when we all moved to California. After Dan and I moved back to Ohio, we visited them frequently in California, and when Erica came along, she immediately fit in with the group. She became the child they never had. Ellen was fond of saying, "Every girl needs something from Tiffany's," and she made certain that Erica got her share.

Every summer we spent a week with Dave and Ellen on Lake Dunmore in Vermont near where Ellen spent her summers as a child. The cabin was so poorly constructed that you could see light through the boards, and although it did have running water, the water was pumped from the lake so it wasn't suitable for anything but bathing and flushing. The cabin was furnished with a mishmash of ancient and uniformly uncomfortable upholstered furniture, which always smelled of mildew, but the accommodations didn't matter. We spent the days in ferocious water-fights or visiting the Ben and Jerry's factory or at Fourth of July festivities in tiny Brandon. It was a magical time for all of us to be children again.

Except for Joerdie and Eric, and Jim Bowsher, Dave and Ellen were our closest friends. We were all devastated when the melanoma returned because we didn't know about sacred contracts. I only knew that when Ellen passed over, I was going to be there to help both her and Dave in whatever way I could. The fact that I had a demanding full-time job didn't matter to me. I was going to California with or without company approval. I knew Dave and Ellen would have done the same for either of us.

Darrel was extremely supportive. We agreed that when Dave called to say caring for Ellen was more than he could do alone, I would head for San Jose and not return until after the funeral, however long that might be. In late August 1996, I called Ellen.

Although she was obviously trying to sound strong, her voice was tired and weak.

"So how are you doing?"

"Oh, I'm fine. Just a little tired, but other than that, I'm fine."

"That's great. Do you want me to come out?"

"Oh, no. That isn't necessary. Dave is handling everything OK. We're fine."

"I'm glad to hear it. Why don't you let me talk to him for a minute?"

When Dave came to the phone, it was immediately obvious that everything was far from fine.

"How are you really doing?" I asked.

"We're doing OK."

"Is Ellen still able to be up and around and take care of herself?"

Silence. "Not really."

"Is she still ambulatory?"

"No. Not really. I have to help her to the bathroom. Other than that she pretty much stays on the sofa."

"Do you want me to come out now?"

He hesitated, clearly torn. "No. You have your family and your job. We're managing OK."

"Did Ellen tell you not to ask me for help? Look, Dave, I've made all of the arrangements with work. As soon as you say the word, I'm coming out, and I'm staying until the end."

He responded, "Come now."

I flew out the next day, not knowing exactly what to expect. The situation was worse than I had anticipated. Ellen was no longer able to climb the stairs at all and was dividing her time between the sofa in the upstairs family room and her bed. She was no longer strong enough to walk unassisted to go to the bathroom or even pull herself up from the sofa. Always a large woman, even after losing fifty pounds from the cancer, she still weighed about 250 pounds. It was an effort for Dave and me to even pull her to her feet.

I immediately set out to make the living arrangements more comfortable and organized. Organizing is what I do in times of extreme stress. Dave had been preparing meals, such as they were, in the kitchen downstairs and carrying them up to Ellen. She sat on the sofa with her tray of food on the coffee table in front of her. Dave continued to eat his meals in the kitchen. I suggested that we bring a table and chairs up to the family room so that we could all eat together and maintain at least a semblance of normalcy although things were well beyond the point of normal.

With her condition deteriorating daily, Ellen was frustrated and angry. Used to being in control, she now found herself having no control over anything in her life, but she still tried. The day before her childhood friend Jane arrived, I cleaned the guest bathroom, put out clean yellow towels from the linen closet filled with clean yellow towels, and got Jane's room ready for her. Later I saw Dave scurrying around in a state of near-panic

"They don't match!"

"What do you mean they don't match? What doesn't match?"

"The towels. They don't match."

"They're all exactly the same color. How could they not match?"

"The little trimmy stuff on the edge is different. I have to change them."

I discovered Ellen sitting in the guest bathroom directing Dave to change all the towels. She couldn't get to the bathroom by herself, so Dave had to help her there so she could inspect our work. Our explanation that Jane wouldn't care what towels were out didn't matter. Ellen needed to be in control of something, no matter how inconsequential.

There were lighter, poignant moments during those weeks. When Jane arrived, she pulled three large, brightly decorated hats from her suitcase and announced that we were going to have a tea party. We helped Ellen out of her gown and into street clothes, applied her makeup, and helped her to the table. The three of us, wearing Jane's hats, had a party with tea and cookies served on the china tea set that had been Ellen's grandmother's, just as Jane and Ellen had done as children together. We laughed and cried as Dave caught the scene on film. When she passed over, Dave gave the tea set to Jane as Ellen requested.

When her mother and stepfather passed over, Ellen used some of her inheritance to buy a retreat near the ocean in Pacific Grove. She loved the house because it was a sanctuary from her high-powered job where she handled the mergers and acquisitions for a large international telecommunications company. The house was her sacred space, but when Ellen insisted that she wanted to see it one last time, we had no idea how we could honor her request. She hadn't been downstairs for more than a month, and even getting her up one step and the few yards to the bathroom was an incredible ordeal. They had a wheelchair left over from her mother's illness, but there were still the stairs to contend with. Finally, we helped Ellen to the top of the long staircase, where she managed to sit down. She slowly descended the stairs on her bottom, one step at a time. At the bottom, we helped her into the wheelchair and wheeled her to the waiting car.

Once at Pacific Grove, unable to walk more than a few steps under her own power, we dragged Ellen up the two steps and into the house, where all she could do was sit a few minutes and feel the energy of the place she loved most. We got her back into the car and drove to the ocean a few blocks away. It was early evening, and the air was brisk as it blew over the water. We helped Ellen back into the wheelchair and wheeled her onto the soft sand, wrapped in a blanket to protect her from the cold. She stared out at the ocean, sobbing, knowing it was the last time she would see it in this lifetime.

Finally back at San Jose, we were all exhausted, and Ellen was too weak to ascend the stairs the way she had come down. Even with the three of us pushing, pulling, and lifting, we couldn't get her up the stairs. Finally in desperation we called the fire department, which sent a crew of burly men to carry Ellen up to her bed. By the time they arrived, she was sobbing from the humiliation of having total strangers see her in such a predicament and from the realization that her health was deteriorating so rapidly.

Jane left the next morning, and Dave called hospice to evaluate our situation. The volunteer immediately determined that Ellen's condition was even more dire than we realized. She ordered a hospital bed and bedside commode. From that point on, Ellen never left the bed in the family room again except to use the commode.

Friends from all periods of Ellen's life began coming to see her. Although she appreciated the visits, she began referring to them as the death watch. When the phone rang, before we could answer it, Ellen would call out, "Is she dead yet?" in anticipation of the caller inquiring about her condition. We didn't know if we should laugh or cry, and at times we did both.

Because of her size and the fact that she was losing strength so rapidly, getting Ellen out of bed and onto the commode and then back into bed took all our strength. It was only a matter of days until she slipped out of our arms and onto the floor. No matter what we tried, Dave and I could not get her to her feet and back into bed. We once again called the fire department, and when the same crew arrived, we joked about Ellen's new friend Officer Garcia. It wasn't funny though, because we knew it was the last time she would be out of bed. The next morning the hospice volunteer inserted a catheter and brought a bed pan. She also brought liquid morphine, which would become crucial to Ellen's existence the remainder of her earthwalk.

While I was willing to do anything, Dave and I soon discovered that I could not handle anything he dubbed "gaggy." Unfortunately, that included almost anything involving a bodily function. Giving Ellen her bath pushed the limits of what I could do. I would gag just trying to hold the pan into which she spit toothpaste water.

I cooked nondescript meals everyday; it didn't matter that they were boring and tasteless because none of us felt like eating. I also did the laundry, but not to Ellen's satisfaction. Literally on her deathbed, she was still trying to teach me the proper way to fold fitted sheets. We laughed because we both knew that as soon as she wasn't looking, I would go back to my normal method of wadding the fitted sheet into a ball and placing it under the neatly folded top sheet in the linen closet. When she was awake, I sat beside Ellen's bed and read from her favorite books or talked about happier times, like the summers spent in Vermont. In the evening, Dave and I would sip Bacardi and Coke while he vented his anger and frustration. Sometimes he would sob and pound his fists. I knew exactly how he felt, watching the only person he had ever loved slipping away before his eyes and being powerless to stop it. However, when I arrived in San Jose I began doubling my daily dose of Prozac, so I was detached and unemotional. I was aware of what was happening, but too numb to react. It was a mixed blessing. I was once again stuffing my emotions, but it did help to have one of us remain relatively calm.

Dave especially was pushed to the human breaking point, and we tried to find humor amidst the chaos. One morning, hearing a loud thud, I raced to the family room afraid that Ellen had rolled out of bed. Instead I found Dave sprawled on the floor beside the over- turned recliner, in which he had attempted to sleep. He was wearing white briefs and an undershirt, surgical stockings for his phlebitis, a cervical collar for his aching neck, and a mouth guard to prevent him from grinding his teeth. His long, dark hair was standing on end. He looked so pathetic that we couldn't help but laugh at the depth to which he had sunk to survive this ordeal in which he had agreed to participate. We also joked that should Ellen have awakened and seen that sight, it might have hastened her passing.

"Man, I didn't sleep at all last night. Ellen was restless, and I was up with her all night. I finally decided to sleep in the chair so I didn't have to keep running back and forth. I had just drifted off to sleep when the chair tipped over."

"Why didn't you wake me to take a turn?"

"Well, I couldn't." He laughed. "Everything was gaggy."

Within days, Ellen lost the ability to swallow, which meant that she could no longer take the medications that kept her brain from swelling and her organs from shutting down. We knew the end was near. Early the next morning, with the two of us at her bedside, Ellen quietly passed over. She was forty-seven.

Dave and I began calling friends. We made funeral arrange- ments according to Ellen's wishes. In typical, efficient Ellen fashion, she had chosen her clothes and picked a caterer and menu. She loved to entertain, and wanted to be sure that her last big party was a success. She also requested that Dan sing at her funeral, a request he was going to find difficult to honor without breaking down.

Several out-of-town friends, including Dan and Erica, arrived to visit Ellen only to discover that they would instead be attending her funeral. In all, Dave had seven houseguests camping out in his home, which broke the tension of realizing Ellen was gone. We were Ellen's best friends, from all phases of her life, yet many of us had never met each other before. We spent the next several days sharing our favorite Ellen stories and bonding together in our common grief.

The funeral service was beautiful, as one might expect from any function Ellen planned. I was still eerily void of emotion and only broke down briefly, when Dan sang Dave and Ellen's favorite song, Simon and Garfunkel's "For Emily, Wherever I May Find Her." Dave asked three of us to speak at the service, representing the significant phases of Ellen's life. Jane, who had known Ellen since they were small children spoke first, talking about walking to nursery school together and having sleepovers. Susan knew Ellen as an astute, no-nonsense business woman from their years together at the telecommunications company. I mentioned our days at Ohio University, when we were groupies of the campus rock band in which Dan and Dave were members. But I talked mostly about our summers in Vermont, where Ellen and I, both large women, would tap dance together, much to Erica's horror. And I told how we would walk down the quiet streets of Middlebury, doing the Monkee walk and singing "Great Green Gobs of Greasy, Grimy Gopher Guts." It was a side of Ellen most people never got to experience.

I stayed an extra two days after the other people went home. Dave and I had been through a lot together in the previous weeks, and we both needed to decompress and process what had occurred. The house had been full of laughter and excitement with all the guests; now it was deadly silent. We spent those two days watching home movies of Ellen—little Ellen Sue, as she was known then—as a small child hopping, jumping, and running across the grainy film. It was hard to comprehend that she was gone.

I left on Monday, knowing that on Tuesday I would be back at my desk trying to act as if everything was fine and nothing had changed. But nothing was fine, and everything had changed. The Prozac enabled me to keep going, but I was in deep emotional trouble. I was, after all, a victim.

As if the Universe hadn't provided enough drama, as I sifted through the back issues of the local newspaper that accumulated the month I was away, I discovered that Dave Ullery had passed over while I was gone. I knew he had been fighting kidney dis-ease for several years, but I had no idea it was life threatening. He was sixty-three.

Even with the Prozac, between interviews I would frequently close my office door and sob, or call my friend in Detroit whose life always seemed to be in more crisis than mine. A conversation with him on any given day was guaranteed to bring me down further, which was what I wanted when I was in victim mode.

Although I understood how to play the corporate game, I always

found it to be phony and distasteful, so I avoided it as much as possible. I worked hard, did my job well, and had no aspirations to rise
higher in the corporate ranks. Now in the wake of losing more
people I loved, I was so deeply ensconced in victim mode that I
could no longer bring myself to even pretend to play the game. I
understood life and death, and what I was doing at Copeland was not
life and death. When I was in a downward spiral, such as when I
killed Harley, my behavior became self-destructive. I found myself
doing things that were nothing short of reckless, yet I appeared
unable to stop. For example, a secretary who had worked for
Manager A for several years bid on a secretarial position with
Manager B in another department. Manager B called me to talk
about the secretary and her qualifications.

"Tell me about her. Why does she want to leave Manager A?"

"She's probably just ready for a change. She has excellent test
scores. Everyone in her department seems to really like her. Your
department is more exciting than what she's doing now. She's an
excellent candidate."

"No. Come on. Give me the real dirt. Why does she want to
leave Manager A?"

Normally I am capable of tact and finesse, but in this case, I
could muster neither, opting instead for truth.

"Because he treats her like crap!" I blurted out.

Manager B immediately called Manager A, who in turn called
Darrel. Darrel, who is always tactful, tried to smooth the ruffled
feathers my outburst caused and at the same time appropriately reprimand me. Unfortunately, he found it very difficult to reprimand a
near-zombie who no longer cared if she even had a job. At the time
I didn't remember with any certainty what I had said to either
manager.

The poor secretary did not receive the job with Manager B and
was forced to continue working for Manager A, who now knew how
she really felt about him. Even through she chose the experience as
part of her sacred contract, I can't imagine her human life improved.
Nothing happened to me, but I knew it was time for me to go.

The Universe stepped in and provided two opportunities to
facilitate my departure. In January, Dan became President and CEO
of the family business. The accompanying salary increase made my

income much less significant. We decided that I would stay until the end of the school year and then quit so that Erica and I could spend the entire summer at our cottage in Michigan. I only hoped that I could last that long without completely falling apart.

Within weeks I heard through the rumor mill that another employee in the department was about to be laid off. He had a wife and children, and I already knew I was going to resign in a few more weeks. I talked with Darrel.

"I heard a rumor that so-and-so is going to be laid off. Is it a performance issue or strictly headcount? If it's only headcount, I might be willing to take a voluntary layoff in his place."

"It's a little of each," he responded. "How did you hear about it? It's supposed to be confidential."

"You know nothing is secret around here," I said. "Actually I heard it from his manager."

"Man, she shouldn't do that. What if he found out before we told him? That would be awful."

"I haven't discussed it with anyone but you; I thought if I could save his job, I didn't mind doing it. My career is certainly not going anywhere now."

Darrel hesitated. "They're still going to want to lay him off, but I might be able to help you. Nobody knows this yet, so you can't say anything. I've accepted a promotion with the company in Chicago. I'm going to be leaving in about a month. I don't know who your new manager will be or what you'll be up against. If you're serious about leaving, I'll see what kind of deal I can get for you."

Dan and I were delighted by the prospect of an unexpected severance package. I was planning to leave the company anyway, so anything they offered was a bonus. Darrel came back to me with an offer, and I left the company in June, as planned.

A few months later, the Tri-County NAACP honored me with the Martin Luther King, Jr. Friendship Award for my work in hiring and promoting minorities during my time at Copeland. I was touched almost beyond words. As I said in my acceptance speech, I didn't know they gave awards for just doing what is right. I was the first woman to receive the honor. The recipient before me was the former President of Copeland. It was one of the greatest honors of my life.

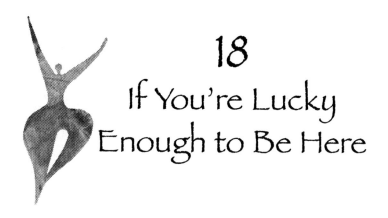

18
If You're Lucky
Enough to Be Here

Erica and I headed north to the cottage in Michigan as soon as school was out for the summer. She got a job scooping ice cream at the tiny market, a half-mile up the road from the cottage. When she wasn't working, she hung out with friends from the nearby cottages. These friends were, for the most part, the children of the people Dan and his brothers and sister hung out with when they were her age. There are few rules for teenagers on the lake, primarily because they are contained by their surroundings. There was no place to go without a car, other than the tiny market which closed at dark, and none of these kids was old enough to drive. They were free to stay out until all hours. This was Erica's first taste of independence, so I didn't see her much except when our cottage was the designated gathering place.

The lake has been a favorite spot for the Fischer family since the turn of the century when Dan's grandparents discovered it. They must have known it was there, because at the time the area where they bought property was only accessible by horse and wagon or boat. They built their first cottage in the early 1900s and it remained, with modifications, until 1978. Among the family members, I was most thrilled with the new cottage because it sported two and one-half baths, as opposed to the old house with its extremely small septic system and one bathroom. Not having grown up on a lake, even a pristine one, I was appalled when Dan's mother suggested that I take my bar of Ivory (it floats) and bathe in the lake.

She didn't understand that the lake was precisely what I was hoping to wash off.

That was the same summer she tried to teach me to make mayonnaise from the egg yolks left over from the egg whites she used to make the angel food cake from scratch. I was only a few years beyond salmon casserole from the Bland but Grand Cookbook, and I could see no sense in wasting time making something that tasted to me like Hellmann's. But, wanting to get along, I grudging agreed to learn the sacred ritual. We stirred and mixed, and did whatever it is you're supposed to do to homemade mayonnaise, and it simply wasn't coming together. Finally, in frustration, Janet turned to me and screamed, "You're the dumbest thing I've ever seen!" That set the tone for the relationship for the next several years. We obviously chose an interesting contract together.

With the construction of the new cottage, things at the lake improved dramatically. Unlike the old cottage, there were real bedrooms with doors and ceilings, replacing the seven foot-high-partitions with cardboard accordion doors. Best of all, I was never again invited to help with the mayonnaise.

The cottage is in a beautiful, serene place, on a lake with crystal-clear water and very little boat traffic. Our friends Bob and Susie Nolan have a plaque on the wall of their cottage that describes it perfectly. "If you're lucky enough to be here, you're lucky enough." I felt lucky indeed. In all the years I worked outside the home, I never reached the point where it wasn't an effort to drag myself out of bed in the morning. Now, away from the stresses of my job, I had absolutely no restraints on my time. I could sleep all day if I wanted, but instead many mornings I found myself sitting under a huge oak tree in the front yard, watching the sun rise over the lake. I was so relaxed that I soon cut my Prozac dosage in half, back to what it was before Ellen passed over.

It worked out well for Dan that Erica and I were gone. He was free to work long hours without feeling as though he was neglecting us. For my part, I could enjoy my freedom without feeling that I had abandoned him. We talked by phone several times a day, and he tried to come up for a long weekend every other week. It was a good summer for all of us.

That was also the summer I learned to read for pleasure; by the time fall rolled around, I had read almost every book on *The New York Times* best seller list. I didn't venture out much to meet the other people on the lake. Instead, when I wasn't reading, I rented and watched every new release at the local Blockbuster. It was exactly what I needed to begin my emotional healing.

Back in Wapakoneta at the end of the summer, we moved into Dan's parents' house, where Dan and all his siblings spent their childhoods. Lucas had passed over two years before, and Janet, in the latter stages of Alzheimer's dis-ease, was in a nursing home. Erica was reluctant to leave because we had moved into our old house just in time to celebrate her first birthday. It was the only home she knew, and she didn't want to leave all those childhood memories. It was a good move for the family, though. The house was larger, and had a huge backyard bordering the Auglaize River. Over the years, Lucas planted many varieties of trees, so that sitting on the deck over-looking the yard became as close to paradise as one could find in the city.

19
Help From a Ninja

As the time grew closer for my flashbacks to begin, the Universe assisted in remarkable ways to prepare me. Many powerful beings, some in human form such as Joerdie, and others in spirit, began helping me prepare for my journey. Few have had a greater or more dramatic impact on my earthwalk than a young man named Ian Fisher.

Joerdie and Eric were blessed with two amazing sons, Ian and Scott. These new parents learned quickly that their boys were special. Ian was only six months old when to Joerdie and Eric's surprise, the infant turned to Eric, smiled, and said clearly, "Hi, Dad!" By nine months, Ian was speaking in full sentences. When Ian and Scott announced that they saw spirits in their rooms or heard voices, Joerdie, unlike most parents, encouraged them to develop their gifts and thus the boys were both extremely psychic from infancy. Ian especially knew when things were going to happen, saw auras, and heard things most of us could only imagine.

One evening hearing an unusual commotion, Joerdie went to investigate just as Ian rushed from his room.

"Hurry up, Mom. I finally got all the spirits into the closet. Now you tell them to shut up so I can get some sleep."

Both ornery and fun loving, Ian was about twelve when he concocted a particularly fine prank and got caught. Quickly pulling the hood of his sweatshirt tight around his face until only his eyes were visible, Ian proclaimed in the worst possible Asian accent, "I am a neenja. I moost not be seen in pooblic!" as though his "invisibility" would somehow render him less culpable for the crime. His ploy worked because his parents were laughing too hard to consider punishing him. From that time on, anything unexplained was attributed to "the ninja." Such was the case when the minister at the church we all attended received an unusual request in the collection plate. Among the weekly donations was a note from a mysterious stranger named Zing Wan Xan, requesting that the minister call on him. Coincidentally Xan's address and telephone number were the same as Ian's because Zing Wan Xan was his cat.

Both a fine musician and artist, Ian moved to Denver to attend art school. He settled there permanently after he married and his daughter was born. Ian devoted much of his time to working with troubled youth, helping, and in some cases, supporting young people, many of whom were runaways. He helped them get off alcohol and drugs, and once they were clean, Ian helped them find jobs or hired them to work for him in his home-painting business. When the homeless shelters in Denver were full, Ian frequently took in the overflow, ensuring that the people had a safe place to stay.

Since he was a young boy, Ian had had a premonition about his own passing. He told Joerdie that he knew that he would not live past twenty-five, and that he would die in a fire. Apparently Ian was already aware of his sacred contracts.

In the early morning of December 17, 1997, while Joerdie and Eric were in Colorado visiting, an angel appeared to Joerdie in a dream. The angel took the form of our friend Mary Ann with whom Joerdie had been having deep conversations about their growing spiritual beliefs for several years. In the dream the angel said to Joerdie, "Remember the things we have been talking about. There are three things I want you to meditate on today: Death is never an accident; there are no coincidences, and only love is real." When she awoke, Joerdie meditated.

Later that day, Ian's house exploded, caught fire, and burned to the ground. His wife escaped unharmed, but Ian was badly burned. Their two-year-old daughter was with Joerdie and Eric at the time. When Eric called the University of Denver emergency room, the doctor told him that Ian's injuries were fatal, and that as soon as his wife was able to accept the fact that Ian was gone, they would disconnect the life support. When Joerdie and Eric arrived at the hospital, Ian had passed over. At the time of his passing, Ian was twenty-four.

When Joerdie and Eric returned to Lima following Ian's memorial service, she discovered a book she had ordered had arrived. As Joerdie began reading *Talking to Heaven* by James Van Praagh, it immediately resonated with her, validating what she already knew: death of the physical body is not the end of the life. She carried the book with her everywhere she went, dozens of yellow Post-It notes marking the particularly significant pages, numerous passages underscored or highlighted, the book dog-eared from constant use. She recommended it to everyone she met, and frequently gave copies to friends.

When I read the book, shortly after Joerdie, it changed my life. While I always believed in reincarnation, Van Praagh's book was incredibly powerful in detailing his encounters with spirits who had passed over to the other side. I finally understood that we are powerful spiritual beings, participating in a human experience. I immediately began reading other spiritual books, usually ones that Joerdie recommended, including *Echoes of the Soul* by Echo Bodine, and *Seat of the Soul* by Gary Zukav, and with each one I finished, the Universe tilled the soil and planted the seeds of my spiritual journey, preparing me for my own major revelation.

Not long after he passed over, Ian began working with his loved ones on this plane. Strange phenomenon such as lights going on and off by themselves and objects moving across the room became the norm at the Fisher house. Joerdie was soon able to hear Ian and other spirits, frequently children. Ian told her that he was still working with young people, but now on the other side. Most had agreed to experience abuse in their most recent human earthwalks; many had completed suicide. Ian worked with them by helping them to make the transition to the next dimension. I believe it was Ian's constant prompting that eventually helped me release my own memories of the abuse I agreed to experience.

Erica and I headed to Michigan again in June, six months after Ian's passing. This time I was reading *Book of the Hopi*, a book on the history and traditions of the Hopi Indians, which immediately struck a chord with me. I discovered a store run by Native Americans, which featured art and jewelry, but more importantly books and music. I began reading everything I could get my hands on regarding Native tradition and listening to Native American music. I was particularly intrigued by the work of Jamie Sams, who in addition to several excellent books, compiled a tarot-like set of cards called *Sacred Path Cards: the Discovery of the Self through Native Teachings*. As I read the material, I began doing the exercises in the accompanying workbook and found I had a genuine connection to the Native American teachings. They felt much closer to my personal beliefs than what I found around me in the rest of the world. For example, rather than viewing people with different sexual orientations as perverse, Native Americans actually revered them, recognizing them as more balanced between their male and female sides than heterosexuals. I also read that anything that helps an individual is medicine.

With that in mind, as I began learning to meditate, I also began smoking small amounts of marijuana almost daily—but only for the medicinal value, of course. Although I had smoked it intermittently since the late '60s, I hadn't smoked pot for several years, probably since I began working for Copeland. Every day I sat on the screened porch overlooking the lake, burning incense, stoned, and trying to meditate. Not only couldn't I quiet the normal voices in my head, I met entirely new ones whose message seemed to be "Go eat those cookies, man." So as I tried to seek enlightenment, I instead numbed myself further with marijuana and Prozac. While I didn't reach Nirvana, I learned a lot from all the reading I was doing, which continued to prepare me for what was about to happen for me.

Section Four:
AHA!

20
Oh, Thank God!

I will never forget the day I began to remember. It was late October, just after my forty-ninth birthday. I was in my living room with Joerdie when I glanced at a picture of my father. He was a small man of Norwegian descent with sandy brown hair and pale blue eyes. Most people found the picture to be eerie. While the face was smiling, the eyes were wild, filled with fear. I usually found comfort in the picture, but this time I saw something different.

I turned to Joerdie and blurted out, "Do you think my dad sexually abused me?"

The question was absurd because it seemed to come out of nowhere, but as soon as the words poured out of my mouth, I knew that they were true.

To my amazement she shrieked, "Oh, thank God! You finally remember!" Obviously neither of us knew about sacred contracts at the time.

Joerdie told me a bizarre story that had taken place nearly a decade before when she was asked to serve on a board that provided services for people who agreed to experience a lifetime of sexual abuse. As part of the literature from the group, she received a checklist of the behavior people who have experienced sexual abuse frequently exhibit. As she read the list aloud to Eric, she became increasingly alarmed.

"Pattern of being a victim (victimizing oneself after being victimized by others), especially sexually; no sense of own power or right to set limits or say no; pattern of relationships with much older persons (onset in adolescence).' Oh, my God, Eric, that's Nancy," she said.

"Depression (sometimes paralyzing). Suicidal thoughts, attempts, obsession (including passive suicide).' Oh, my God, Eric, that's Nancy!" she said again, her alarm and certainty growing with each symptom she read.

Joerdie wasn't a trained professional, only a loving friend deeply concerned for my well-being. As such, she decided to confront me with her suspicions. Standing in my kitchen as I began to cook dinner one evening, Joerdie approached me gingerly about my father. Apparently it wasn't gingerly enough because, I became so angry that I picked up a skillet and threw it at her. I say "apparently," because, as with so many incidents in my life, I still have no memory of the event. People who have chosen to experience traumatic human events learn to dissociate or separate themselves from the events. They block out the memories that are too painful to remember as a defense to help them survive the human trauma. Sometimes the memories are buried for entire lifetimes, with the participants never remembering. Other times, as in my case, the memories will pour out spontaneously or will be triggered by some other event after being buried for decades.

Since I still have no first-hand memory of my kitchen encounter with Joerdie, when I began writing this book, I asked her to describe what happened after I threw the skillet.

"After you threw the skillet, it was as if it had never happened, at least from your actions. You talked to me with your back to me for a while in a very even, weirdly calm voice. As I recall, you got out another pan and began to fry beef for tacos. I don't remember being angry, only confused. You were textbook according to the pamphlet, and the more I read on the subject, the more I was sure of it. I had never been comfortable around your dad. When I went home, I told Eric that it was hard to believe that in all the years of therapy you hadn't been asked that question. Little did I know that you had."

Having learned a painful lesson, Joerdie never broached the subject again; she instead waited patiently for ten years, hoping that my own memories would return.

21
Emotional Jello-O

After the initial memory, I began having flashbacks of the abuse I agreed to experience and the other events in my childhood that had previously not made sense. Sometimes they would appear as a quick glimpse, like a slide flashing across a white screen. Other times entire scenes would play out in my mind's eye. Prone to nightmares of monsters and of being chased since early childhood, now my dreams were becoming vivid and dramatic. Even smells began to trigger memories. I remember picking up our friend Jim Bowsher to go to a concert, when he handed me a book of poetry by Dorothy Parker. The book had been in his garage for a long time, and as I opened it, the smell of mildew immediately triggered memories of the paperback sex novels my father kept in the musty basement of my childhood home. As soon as I opened the poetry book and smelled the mildew, I burst into tears.

The first weeks after the flashbacks began were the most traumatic from the human standpoint, because I was having feelings and memories that I had not experienced for decades. Dan and I stayed close to home, venturing out only when necessary and seeing only our closest friends—Joerdie, Eric, and Jim. Everything felt different, because it was. I spent my entire life as a victim, but this was enormous compared with anything else I had ever experienced.

At times the memories would come pouring in and I would be reduced to emotional Jell-O. One night after dinner at Joerdie's, Jim made some off-hand remark as he is prone to do in even the best of circumstances that completely threw me for a loop. His remark wasn't cruel or even intrusive; but it triggered an unexpected emotional response. I didn't burst into hysterical sobbing; instead I wandered off into Ian's old room, where I cried myself to sleep at the foot of his bed huddled in the fetal position.

Everything felt new and foreign, because I wasn't accustomed to feeling at all. After years of suppressing my feelings with fear and drugs—both legal and illegal—my raw emotion was now exposed. I liken it to a man blind from birth suddenly having his sight restored. Just as he must train his eyes to decipher the new stimuli they are receiving until they focus and produce clear images, I was struggling to make sense of the feelings and information that were flooding in. I was ill-equipped to handle the sudden barrage.

I was always adept at hiding my feelings behind a smiling façade and quick joke, but that didn't work anymore. I was forced to face my feelings. When I would venture out in public, I began indiscriminately telling casual acquaintances things that I remembered. It was bizarre. My father was a civic leader in our small community. People also knew that I adored him, and continued to adore him, yet here I was telling this crazy story of sexual abuse to almost anyone who would listen. I felt the need to purge the memories bottled up, but I felt an even more compelling need to reconcile the memories I was now discovering with the memories of the father I had always adored.

While I didn't yet know about sacred contracts, I had been studying enough spiritual books to understand that everything happens for a reason. I couldn't imagine what the purpose could possibly be, and I was extremely conflicted emotionally between my emerging spiritual beliefs and the human experience that always resulted in my choosing to be a victim.

22
The Very Dark Room

I had very few memories of my childhood before age twelve, a common trait among people who have agreed to experience incest. The memories I did have, which would seem bizarre to almost anyone else, I accepted as a normal part of my childhood.

I always knew about my father's extensive pornography collection. An amateur photographer, he had turned our cellar's old coal bin into his darkroom ostensibly for the purpose of developing photographs. He spent a lot of time in there behind a closed door, but we never saw many results, at least in the way of family photos.

The darkroom was aptly named. Even though its use in developing film was somewhat limited, at least from the human perspective, the secrets it concealed were indeed dark. In this tiny cinderblock room, which always remained locked, my father housed his vast collection of pornographic material including pictures, magazines, books, and sexual paraphernalia of all types. As a very small child, I remember magazines with pictures of people in nudist camps carrying on every day activities totally naked. I was fascinated. A fastidious woman, my mother would sometimes clean the house nude (presumably to prevent her clothes from getting dirty), but I could scarcely imagine her playing volleyball on the front lawn with the neighbors as the people in the pictures were doing, totally devoid of clothing. When I asked my dad where the people came from, he always replied, "Denmark," and I remember thinking what an interesting place Denmark must be.

The volleyball courts of Denmark were a far cry from the majority of places my dad's collection visited. Most of the photographs were the same gray, grainy quality that my father produced in his darkroom, and were of men, women, children and animals engaged in all manner of sexual activity. None of the pictures seemed shocking to me at the time; of course, I had no knowledge of either sacred contracts or the human concept of right and wrong. It would be decades before I would come to understand that all of these beings on Classroom Earth were volunteers and that nothing could ever occur that they did not agree to experience for the lessons they came to learn.

Even though the darkroom remained locked, my dad showed me where he hid the key on a high ledge outside the room. I was so small at the time that I had to drag a chair over to retrieve it. I was not only permitted to look at the material, I was encouraged to look at it when he wasn't home. A bright, curious child, I devoured his paperback sex novels the way most children of the day read Nancy Drew and The Bobbsey Twins. I was already reading when I entered kindergarten, the result, no doubt, of Charlie Zaenglein's mentoring, but if I didn't understand a word or concept in the book, my father was more than happy to explain.

I could look at my father's books and pictures, but I could never tell anyone, especially my mother. This was our special secret. From the human standpoint, I'm certain my father was trying to prevent her from learning about the sexual abuse that was part of our sacred contract. His concern was human judgment. This is also how he began to encourage mistrust between my mother and me by manipulating our relationship. Our contracts were complex, the result, I believe, of many lifetimes working together.

My relationship with my mother was, at best, tumultuous. I learned early in life not to engage her in anything more than the most superficial of conversations. I never knew what would send her into a rage, and I was not willing to take the risk. When she complained that the family kept secrets from her, she was correct. Jealously and insecurity were lessons my mother worked on throughout this earthwalk, and keeping secrets from her drove her human ego crazy. It did, however, provide her soul with the opportunity to work on the lessons. I only knew the human perspective, not the spiritual cause of the behavior, so I chose, for the most part, to make her irrelevant in my life.

By the time I entered high school, my confrontations with my mother reached the point of physical violence. Typically Mother would say something to me, and I would respond in a typical teenage manner, laughing at her or mocking her. Then it began. She would start swinging at me and try to pull my hair. I had the advantage of youth and strength, so when she would strike out at me, I would grab one of her wrists in each hand, holding her stationery. Unable to hit me, she would sputter obscenities at me through clenched teeth, face growing red with fury. Occasionally she would manage a couple of nasty kicks to my shins, but generally she was unable to touch me. As she grew more enraged, I laughed and taunted her more which only made her angrier. Eventually my father would step in and physically separate us although he never actually took sides. Since he was the adult, not taking her side was, in essence, siding with me. I knew there would be no consequences.

I thought all mothers and daughters engaged in physical confrontations. I knew that none of my friends particularly liked their parents at that age, and I didn't know if their disputes erupted into violence. As with so many events in my life, I didn't comprehend what an unusual and complicated relationship we chose.. It may have been what we agreed to in our sacred contracts, but it was still bizarre by human standards.

My relationship with my mother improved to the point of superficial tolerance after Dan and I married. We saw each other only occasionally, usually on holidays. When we were together, we were careful not to talk any more than necessary. After she remarried, we saw her even less. It was a mutual choice.

After the flashbacks began, I had many questions that I hoped she could and would be willing to answer. At that time, I was almost in shock trying to comprehend what my beloved father had done "to" me. I was deep in victim mode and had no comprehension that it was all done for me with my prior consent. How, I wondered, after all those years of never having a real conversation with my mother about anything, would I be able to approach her about something as sensitive as sexual abuse?

The Universe provided the answer. The flashbacks began a few weeks before her birthday, so I invited her to dinner and got her a little drunk. Once she had dropped her guard a bit, I began telling her about my memories, the flashbacks, any bits and pieces that I could remember. I was astounded by her response. The woman who for my entire life would never discuss anything with me at any time, for any reason, looked me in the eye and said, "My God, that makes perfect sense. From the time you were born, it was obvious that he preferred you to me. After you were born, he never wanted to have anything to do with me. It was always you. I hated you for that."

Hearing from your mother that she has always hated you might not be comforting to most people, but for me it was a tremendous gift. I had just received a huge piece of the puzzle. She hated me because I was her rival for my father's affection. He wanted me, not her. She was jealous and she took it out on me in the form of verbal abuse and emotional neglect. It finally made sense. Of course, at the time I had no idea that was our sacred contract.

We talked for several hours and surprisingly her response to everything I told her was unquestioning acceptance. She denied knowing what was happening, but added, "Well, if I had known, what could I have done about it?"

Over the next few months more memories came flooding back, but they were in bits and pieces. As with most people who have agreed to traumatic human experiences such as sexual abuse, I had very few original memories of my first twelve years, and most of what I did remember involved confrontation with my mother.

All of my life I had been searching for answers to the puzzle of my life. Why did I always feel different? Why did I have so much difficulty maintaining relationships, especially with men? I was always depressed to varying degrees. Much of my emotional stability was tied to exterior circumstances. Perhaps I had landed an exciting new job or was heading up a new civic project. Perhaps I had a great new hair color, or maybe I was just really thin. Whatever the exterior source, when the novelty wore off I would sink into a depression deeper than the one before. I went from therapist to therapist desperately seeking answers. They offered few because I wasn't asking the right questions.

Interestingly, almost without exception these counselors asked me early in our relationship whether I had been sexually abused.

When I denied it, none of them pursued the issue further, and so we never discovered the human cause of my behavior. I had no concept that being a victim was a choice I was making and could therefore choose not to make.

Joerdie had been reading metaphysical books for several years which she passed on to me. My spiritual beliefs were changing rapidly, so I made a conscious decision not to seek mainstream psychiatric help when I started remembering. I felt it would be in conflict with my new spiritual beliefs, and I was ready for something new. In addition to the books I was reading, I also began taking metaphysical classes. It was time to look within rather than without for answers. It was the beginning of an exciting journey.

23
I Go Back to Remember

While it is completely normal for children who have chosen to experience traumatic events to block out the memories, I believe my father also employed hypnosis to "help" me forget. Among his possessions when he passed over were stacks of books on hypnosis, and as a child I remember him having a crystal on a chord that he referred to as his "magic amulet" that I would gaze at. He also had some sort of device with a spiral on it that would whirl and render me dizzy. Although I didn't know precisely what he had done to make me forget, I knew I needed professional to help me retrieve my memories. At Joerdie's suggestion I called Susan Fantz, a certified hypnotherapist from New Knoxville, Ohio, who studied regression therapy under noted psychiatrist Dr. Brian L. Weiss. In the days before the appointment, I spent hours meditating and talking to my dad, begging him to help me learn the truth. I held his picture and looked into those wild eyes.

"Hey, how bad can it be?" I asked. "We've been through the worst of it by this time. Let's just wrap up these loose ends and move forward. You need to work with me here. Whatever is still hidden, we can handle."

I had spent years trying to avoid facing my past; now Susan was helping me to remember. As Susan began the meditation, encouraging me to relax and go deep inside myself. I fought it. Even with soft music playing in the background and Joerdie holding my hand for emotional support, rather than relaxing, I became more tense, thoughts swirling in my head. I was terrified of losing control, and so, apparently, was my father. I could feel his presence in the room, dark and fearful, trying to distract me. My father was not a very advanced soul and thus when he left the body, he returned to spirit only at the level of enlightenment that he had reached. He was not suddenly all-knowing. Even though he had left his earthwalk nearly seven years before, my father never embraced the light. Instead he chose to stay in the darkness of fear, and he wanted me remain there with him. Light and dark are simply opposite ends of the same spectrum, as are love and fear. Love is a characteristic of light and fear of darkness. I thought he was afraid of my reaction when I discovered what he had done "to" me. Living in the darkness, and choosing to stay there, he was probably just as reluctant for me to discover what he had done for me because he would no longer be able to control me. I was years away from that awakening. I assured him that everything would be fine, that together we would get through whatever I was about to uncover. I told him I loved him, but that I had to travel down this unknown path in order to heal. At the time I had no idea where it would ultimately take me.

Susan told me to imagine myself walking on a beautiful beach. I saw the beach, but it wasn't beautiful. It was gray, with a cold mist hitting my face and chilling me. The vision was in black and white and more like a scene from a Hitchcock film than the beautiful beach Susan told me to envision. As I walked on the beach, Susan told me I would encounter someone I knew, and asked me to tell her who it was. I saw another person coming toward me and even though I could not see his face, I knew immediately that it was my father. As he walked toward me, I felt his sadness and fear. Susan told me to pick up the pair of scissors that were beside me on the beach. I looked down, and, to my surprise, the scissors were there. I picked them up as she had instructed, but when she told me to cut the cord that connected me to my father, I hesitated, then I argued with her.

"No," I cried, "he's my father. I don't care what he did. I love him."

Susan told me that I had to cut the cord so that he and I could both be free to heal. The scissors were still in my hand, but they were stiff and awkward. Finally I opened the scissors and placed the imaginary cord connecting me to my father between the blades. As I closed the blades, I said, "I love you, Daddy. I release you with love. Go and heal and let me do the same."

Instantly he disappeared, and the beach and ocean were alive with birds and sea creatures. The sun was shining in a blue sky and green waves lapped against the sandy beach. I felt alive and free, eager to jump headfirst into whatever lay ahead.

Susan asked me to climb the stone steps of the cliff by the shore. At the top I saw a big Victorian beach house with a large white porch extending across the front. Susan told me to enter the house and find the stairway that led upstairs.

As I followed Susan's instructions, I was struck by the thought that this was not at all what I expected a regression to be. I expected to be in a deep, coma-like trance, totally unaware of my surroundings. Just the opposite was true. Even though I could see and feel my actions within the meditation, see myself climbing the stairs, I had a heightened awareness of everything outside the meditation as well. I knew exactly where I was and what I was doing. I could hear Susan's calm, reassuring voice and the soft music playing in the background. I could feel Joerdie holding my hand for support. I was an outside observer to all that was happening inside the meditation and without. I realized then that it was a familiar feeling, one that I had used many times before as a child to shield myself from the human trauma of the abuse I had agreed to experience. Once again I had left my body and was now free to watch events unfold.

Leaving the body is a tool the Universe provides to spirits during their human earthwalk for astral travel and also to protect us from the physical and emotional pain of the human trauma the dramas we choose might otherwise produce.

As I climbed the huge wooden staircase in my meditation, Susan told me that when I reached the top, I would see a long hallway with many closed doors. Each door would be numbered, and each number would represent an age. She told me to pick any door I wanted, and, when I was ready, go inside. Without hesitation, I chose door number four.

As I opened the door and stepped inside, Susan asked me to describe what I saw. I was four years old, lying naked on a round bed that was covered with a zebra-striped fake fur spread. There were bright lights encircling the bed and a white screen set up as a background. My father and his friend, another amateur photographer, were there. It was a photo shoot in which I was the star. As I struggled on the bed, my father, naked, forced himself inside me. I screamed and cried while his friend snapped pictures.

"I want my mommy! I want my mommy!" I screamed over and over. "Stop it! It hurts!"

"Your mommy doesn't love you," he said. "Nobody loves you but me. No one will ever love you but me."

"Stop, Daddy! It hurts! It hurts!" I cried, but, of course, he didn't stop until he was finished.

As I dressed, my father said to me, "If you ever tell anyone, I'll kill your kitties."

There were some things in my childhood that I always remembered, but which didn't make sense until my memories began to return. There was an alley along the east side of our house. The bedroom I shared with my sister had a window that looked out on the alley. One Sunday morning I looked out my bedroom window to see my cat Pixie curled up as though sleeping on the other side. I have always been an animal lover, especially cats, and while we always had a multitude of cats, perhaps as many as a dozen, living on and around our back porch, Pixie was one of the few who had occasional house privileges and a name. He was my favorite.

There he was, lying directly in front of my window where it would have been impossible for me not to have found him. Even at that young age, I knew the instant I saw him that he wasn't asleep. I knew he was dead. He didn't have any marks on him, so he obviously hadn't been hit by a car, and he was carefully posed for me to find.

"What do you think happened to him, Daddy?" I asked in tears. "Who would want to hurt my kitty?"

"Probably one of the neighbors poisoned him," he said. My dad never questioned any of the neighbors and never reported the strange death to the authorities. He didn't need to.

We buried Pixie in the back yard under the big box elder tree where we buried all our cats. We wrote his name in chalk on the piece of slate that would serve as a marker until the first rain. Most of the cats only got a description such as "orange tiger" or "big calico." Then the neighborhood children gathered and we sang "Rock of Ages" from an old hymnal, because that was what they did on the 50s television show Wagon Train, when one of the settlers passed over. That was the only experience with death that most of us had at that point in our lives.

We buried Pixie that day, and with him the secret of the abuse I agreed to experience in my sacred contract with my father. I honor Pixie as well as my father for their willingness to participate.

The first regression with Susan lasted for several hours and was emotionally draining for all of us. At times, I would be screaming and crying both in the regression and out. Throughout, Susan's only participation was to ask me to describe what I saw. Prior to this first appointment, Susan and I had never met. She knew only my first name and had no idea why I was coming to see her. She had absolutely no background information about me or my situation. Whatever came out of the regression came from the memories buried deep inside me. None of us, especially me, anticipated the intensity of what I would see and remember, and none of us realized that it was all part of the illusion of Classroom Earth to help me learn the lessons I chose to tackle.

24
Cold Turkey and
Hot Fires

Up to that point, whenever the Universe provided an opportunity I invariably chose the path that allowed me to remain a victim. Following the first regression I had a startling glimpse of my past and, although my first inclination was to play the victim role again, I was beginning to wake up. I was trying to balance on that fine line between being a victim and enlightenment but I found they weren't really compatible. It was time to make definitive changes to eliminate what was not a genuine part of me. While I had used marijuana casually for nearly thirty years, since the flashbacks began it had become a daily ritual. I told myself it was opening my mind to help me remember, when in reality it was just another crutch like the Prozac to keep me numb so that I wouldn't examine my feelings.

In celebration of my fiftieth birthday I decided to eliminate as much that was not genuine from my life as I could handle at that point in my journey. I stopped taking the Prozac, cold turkey and without the guidance of a doctor. I can't emphasize strongly enough that no one should try this. It took several weeks for the drug to work its way out of my system, so I believed initially that I was doing fine without it. I was shocked when after several weeks I began exhibiting withdrawal symptoms: erratic behavior, emotional outbursts, and insomnia. From the human standpoint it was a horrible time for me and everyone around me, but I understand it was all part of the Universal plan. I was tempted to begin the drugs again, but instead I eased the symptoms by taking St. John's Wort and Kava

Kava, drinking herbal teas, and meditating. In time, the withdrawal subsided, and I was clear-headed and drug-free for the first time in thirty years. Initially I was extremely uncomfortable not being numb, but I gradually adjusted.

At the same time I decided to stop dying my hair flaming red. I made the decision to get in touch with my roots; only, after fifteen years, I had no idea what color those roots would be. The red hair was almost my trademark, which was another good reason to eliminate it. My hairdresser at the time told me that many of his clients who were considering going red would use me as the standard. They would either want to be similar to or not as red as Nancy Fischer. Many of my friends had never known me as anything but a redhead, although I can't imagine they thought it was natural.

The intensity of our sacred contract notwithstanding, my mother was really a rather sweet, frightened child terrified of losing her youth and physical beauty. She begged me not to stop coloring my hair because, at almost eighty, she was afraid if her child had gray hair, people might suspect that her own black hair was not natural. When it all grew in, my hair was still primarily dark brown, with only a little white. Drug- and dye-free, I was finally ready to begin exploring who I was, which meant stepping out of my fear. It was a huge step indeed.

I became obsessed with learning or remembering every detail of my past. It was helpful in that the bits and pieces of memories I already had finally made sense. I could remember hiding as a child, but it wasn't until the memories returned that I realized why I was hiding. As I remembered more, I had the opportunity to choose what to do with the information. I could sink deeper into victim mode, or I could begin to step out of my fear. Initially I did a little of both.

After the first regression, I didn't yet know about sacred contracts. My initial reaction was anger toward both my father, who had already passed over, and his photographer friend, who was still living, though in his eighties. When Erica and I returned to Michigan for the summer a few weeks after the regression, I wrote long letters to both my father and his friend, calling them names, swearing at them, venting all of the rage I felt toward them. It was a very human response. I built a fire pit on the shore of the lake, and on the evening of the summer solstice, I made a fire in the pit, said a prayer, and threw the letters in. His friend's letter burned quickly, but my father's letter sputtered amid the flames. It seemed no amount of stirring would get the letter to ignite, almost as if my father was still resisting coming to terms with what he had agreed to do in this lifetime. That was apparently his level of enlightenment when he left this earthwalk, and he had not advanced beyond that point.

It took a long time for my father's letter to be consumed by the purifying flames, but it was extremely empowering for me. To lighten the moment, as the letters burned, I roasted marshmallows and made s'mores. Burning the letters helped me release much of the anger I felt toward my father and his friend. Anger is just a form of fear, so as I began to release this fear, I was a step closer to replacing it with love and light. It was, however, a baby step.

In the fall, just back from Michigan, I was having dinner with Joerdie and Dan at a local downtown restaurant when I looked up to see my father's friend walk past the window outside, his distinctive balding head and Julius Caesar haircut visible above the café-style curtains. It was the first time I had seen him since my regression with Susan and I felt panic when I realized he was about to enter the restaurant. I burst into tears when the hostess seated him and his wife at the next table. For all my work, I was still choosing to be a victim. I got though dinner as best as I could, trying not to look in his direction or establish eye contact, but I knew it would be impossible to get out of the restaurant without stopping to talk with them. He and his wife were close friends of Dan's parents and his daughter was one of my childhood friends.

As we walked by their table on the way out, Dan spoke briefly to the wife. I turned suddenly to my father's friend and said, "Are you still taking a lot of photographs like you did when we were kids?"

He smiled and said, "No, I don't take too many pictures anymore, but thanks for remembering."

At that point I looked him directly in the eyes and said, "I remember a lot of things that you did when we were children."

His face turned ashen white and he slumped noticeably. My ego was very pleased that I caused him discomfort. I told myself I wanted him to think about all the misery he caused all those children and to let him know we were starting to wake up. I actually wanted revenge, a very human phenomenon.

The old man passed over a few years later, the last, I believe, of the group of men who agreed to participate in the abuse drama I chose. I admit my human ego felt relief when he was gone, but from the spiritual standpoint, there is no reason to forgive him or any of the other people who agreed to participate in my drama. Instead, I thank them for their willingness to help my soul advance.

25
It Will All Be
Over in a Minute

Several gifted mediums told me that something major had occurred in my life between the ages of ten and twelve. None were either willing or able to tell me precisely what it was. Undoubtedly it is because our human experiences are about self discovery. If I were going to find out what it was, I had to do it on my own

Since whatever I couldn't remember came up in several readings, I felt it must have been a significant event that I had chosen to experience. I went back to Susan Fantz for another regression.

Susan walked me through the meditation as she had done before, but this time the process was not as long or involved. I no longer needed to visit the beach or cut the cord that connected me to my father. In the intervening months, I had begun meditating more on my own, so it was also easier for me to go into a meditative state.

As I went deep into the meditation, I was with my father, and it was evening. It was a cool, crisp night with lots of stars in the sky, probably in the early fall. I was ten years old. I watched as we drove to a doctor's office, which was closed. My dad knocked on the door and we were quickly greeted by the doctor, in his lab coat, and his wife, who was also his nurse.

The doctor ushered me into one of his examining rooms, handed me a gown, and told me to undress and put it on, which I did without question. When the three adults returned a few minutes later, the doctor instructed me to lie on the examining table with my feet in the metal stirrups. I remember being surprised by the purpose of the stirrups. I had noticed them on my previous visits to the doctor, but I never realized what they were for. In the late '50s, general practitioners handled almost all but the most severe medical problems. The doctor who checked your ears and throat was also likely to deliver your babies and conduct routine pelvic exams, so the stirrups were always there. I felt the heat of the bright light focused on the foot of the table and the discomfort as he inserted the speculum inside my body.

"Yes, she's pregnant, all right," he said.

"You're sure? Well, can you take care of it?" my father asked.

"It will all be over in a minute."

I am not certain whether he administered any type of local anesthetic or not. It seemed to be uncomfortable and although there was some blood, I did not appear to be in any appreciable amount of pain. Of course, it is also likely that I wasn't even in my body at the time.

I left Susan's house, once again amazed at the experiences I agreed to so early in my earthwalk, but souls only agree to what they are able to handle.

I still had many questions. At ten years old, I wondered, how would anyone even have known that I was pregnant? In a reading with my psychic friend Aria Magi of Sedona, she asked my father about the abortion. He confirmed it and also that, as he phrased it, "the seed was his." He told her that the reason he suspected I was pregnant was because over the summer I spent a month with my aunt and uncle in Montana. When I returned in the fall, I had suddenly grown breasts and a large abdomen.

It was following the abortion that the physical portion of my contract with my father ended. Interestingly, because I always chose to be a victim, when the physical contact ended, I felt my father had rejected me. I chose to enter a depression that lasted in varying degrees for nearly forty years.

Section Five:
Alternative Therapies

26
Journeys of Wisdom

After decades of traditional psychotherapy, I intentionally turned to non-traditional and alternative therapies to help guide me through the healing process. Their spiritual natures were more in keeping with my personal beliefs. I began with Journeys of Wisdom.

JOW began as ten three-day workshops and several additional advanced, specialized workshops. The earlier workshops deal mostly with releasing and balancing body energy, in a process called Holistic Kinesiology. Holistic Kinesiology includes the study of all of the natural body energies and their effects at the intuitive, mental, emotional, spiritual, and physical levels. It goes beyond what our conscious bodies and minds perceive as truth, and works to balance the mind, body, and spirit. This sometimes entails uncovering the emotional cause of physical problems and changing the beliefs that caused the problems. It is intense and powerful work.

I attended my first Journeys of Wisdom workshop in Columbus, Ohio, within weeks of my initial flashbacks. As with most of my forays into the spiritual realm, I heard about it through Joerdie. I stress that I attended the workshop rather than participated, because while my physical body occupied space in a chair in the furthest corner of the room, I was hardly present in any other sense of the word.

I did not yet know about sacred contracts, so I was deeply ensconced in being a victim to whom something terrible had happened, rather than understanding that the experiences were for my benefit. Consequently I was having a difficult time comprehending what my beloved father had done "to" me. I still clung desperately to the belief that it could only have been fondling, because I knew that my father would never do anything to hurt me. I was correct, of course, but I didn't understand that I agreed to all of the experiences in our sacred contract. I was also convinced that he acted out of excessive, obsessive love. It was the only motivation I could allow myself to imagine for his actions. Even knowing about the pornography collection, it was inconceivable to me that he had agreed to be a pedophile. While I could say the word "incest," I could not yet comprehend what it meant from the human standpoint, so I certainly didn't understand that from the spiritual standpoint it was a tremendous gift to help my soul evolve. I only knew I was a victim, and a pitiful one at that. This was several months before my first regression with Susan Fantz.

Meanwhile, as my emotions and my memories were struggling to come to the surface, I was still primarily numb, not just from years of repression but from six years of Prozac. Add to the mix that I was still smoking marijuana almost daily, and it is little wonder that I was barely functioning. Every night after the workshop, I sat alone in my hotel room working on my homework exercises, mostly questions that were designed to get me in touch with my feelings, while lighting up a joint whose main purpose was to keep me numb. Because of fear, I chose to delay awakening as long as possible.

People who saw me during that first workshop and then in later ones could barely recognize me as the same person, and it was not just because I had allowed my flaming red hair to return to its natural dark brown. The biggest difference in my physical appearance was my eyes, which were no longer filled with fear, darting wildly back and forth like a cornered animal. The real change came on a soul level as I began to step out of fear and victim energy.

Journeys of Wisdom, founded by John McMullin, provides a very non-threatening environment, which is one of the reasons it is so effective. It was the ideal place for me to be at that critical juncture. From the human standpoint, I was barely hanging on.

Even though the dramas on Classroom Earth are illusions, the trauma of the human experience appears real. I carried a tremendous amount of emotional damage as a result of the abuse I chose to experience. Up to that point, when the Universe provided an opportunity to learn, I always chose the scenario that resulted in me playing the victim role. With the flashbacks and subsequent memories, I had the opportunity to finally begin moving out of that victim energy toward spiritual enlightenment or to have the starring role in the grandest victim drama of my life. Continuing in the victim role was familiar and comfortable.

As with anything in nature, our spiritual journeys are not a straight line. The journey is two steps forward and one step backward so that we are ultimately moving forward. I was moving forward, but I was not so far along that playing the victim again would not have been the easier choice. I did not know about sacred contracts, but I did know that only love is real. Anything that is not love is fear, and while I had plenty of fear, I knew I had to move beyond it. Of course, I had constant encouragement from Joerdie on this plane, and Ian and Dave Ullery on the other side. While the task was going to be enormous, it provided a great opportunity for growth. I had the option to stay where I was on my spiritual journey, but as difficult as it was proving to be, I certainly did not want to come back and do it all again in another lifetime. I decided to plow ahead. I chose Journeys of Wisdom as the first major step in the process.

It was through Journeys of Wisdom that I first learned about the inner children we all harbor, which I believe was one of the most important aspects of my human emotional healing. While I had heard the term "inner child," I didn't realize that they are real and need to be nurtured and protected. The inner children are the parts of our subconscious minds that hold the memories, along with the human illusion of pain and fear, from whatever occurred in our physical lives at any particular age. Because of their past experiences with adults, these inner children are afraid to trust the adults we have become. They don't know about sacred contracts. They only know that adults are not to be trusted. We have to earn the trust of our inner children. Until they feel safe and loved, these inner children will not reveal the knowledge of the past hurts they endured, which we need to know in order to heal our old emotional wounds. That is why my inner children did not come forward with any memories until well after my father, who, from their perspective, abused them, had passed over. They were unwilling to take the risk, because he had demonstrated to them that if they told anyone, he would kill their kitties.

My inner children had very little reason to trust any adult. The two adults they were supposed to be able to trust had proven to be untrustworthy. They did not understand that my soul agreed to all of those experiences and that my parents played their roles in my drama masterfully. Our inner children relate to our human experience while we are in the body, not to the agreements we make before each earthwalk.

The Journeys program taught me how to reach my inner children, sometimes using techniques as simple as crayon drawings that allowed them to express what they remembered in a non-threatening environment, appropriate for their ages. Although the techniques are simple, they are effective, because they allow the children to finally feel empowered rather than victimized, from their purely human perspective.

One level of Journeys of Wisdom, entitled "Awakening the True Self," is unusually intense, as participants learn to examine their past patterns of self-deceptive behavior. Participants study how they control others and how they allow others to control them. They learn to recognize and defuse control dramas that they play with others, which, as they no longer play the games, will lead to self-empowerment. In essence it helps participants become aware of their sacred contracts so that they can begin to dissolve them. One of the goals is to "experience the process of expressing anger and love in a safe environment." This particular workshop is so emotionally draining that, at its completion, participants receive a certificate that reads, "I survived Level 4." I can't reveal exactly what occurs, because each individual's experience is different. It is determined by how far along the spiritual path each person has advanced. There is frequently much screaming and many tears, as participants release their anger, often for the first time in their current earthwalks. I remained totally dry-eyed and very pleased with myself, because I obviously had no anger to release. I was still so numb to my feelings that I couldn't even acknowledge that I carried any anger toward either of my parents. While many who have agreed to experience incest often have intense anger issues, denial is also a primary symptom. My human denial response was still controlling my human anger. My lack of anger at Level 4 was particularly ironic since years later, after many more Journeys of Wisdom workshops and other metaphysical therapy, I was still releasing anger that I carried toward my mother. From a human standpoint, my contract with my mother was much more personal to me than that with my father. It was certainly more complex, probably because she was a more advanced soul than my father. At the time I took Level 4, addressing my anger toward either parent was more than I could bear. I was still so far in denial and numb from the Prozac and marijuana that all I could envision was my father, St. Leo, as some sort of loving protector who adored me just a little too much.

It was during one of these sessions in Level 4 when I asked John, a gifted intuitive, at what point my father had stopped the incest. John's answer stunned and confused me. He said, "The incest never stopped. The physical contact ended when you reached puberty, but the emotional incest is still going on."

I had no idea what he meant, and at that time was too afraid of the answer to ask him for an explanation. He also told me that I had a major traumatic event in my life when I was between ten and twelve, but that my inner children were not ready to release the information to either him or me. He could tell it was there, but could not determine what it was.

It was with that in mind that Joerdie and I set out for my first regression with Susan Fantz. I wanted to know the secret my ten-year old carried, but I wasn't ready. What I found instead was the brave four-year old who showed me the early sexual experiences during the photography sessions, and that St. Leo was not quite so benevolent after all, at least from the human perspective. But it was on the beach, when Susan instructed me to cut the cord that was still connecting me to my father, that I understood what John meant. I was still emotionally tethered to my father, unable to view him in any sort of objective way.

It was not until more than a year later, and after several other mediums told me something major had occurred in my life during that age period, that I went for a second regression with Susan. At that time, my ten-year-old inner child finally came forward and revealed the abortion that I had agreed to, but that she had experienced.

As John has progressed on his spiritual journey, he has restructured the original ten workshops and added many more to reflect and share his new wisdom. Because of this approach, Journeys of Wisdom is always moving forward, just as the participants move forward on their individual journeys.

With the exception of Level 4, Journeys of Wisdom has a gentle and safe, albeit intense, atmosphere. I would often leave the workshop on Sunday night thinking, "Well that was a pleasant enough experience. I met some nice people, but I didn't really learn much." Within a few days I would actually process all that I had taken in during the weekend and finally get the message in the form of a major "Aha!" Every time, it resulted in a leap forward on my spiritual journey. I believe it is this gentle, safe approach, nurturing our frightened inner children, that makes Journeys of Wisdom such a powerful tool, especially for those individuals who are so wounded and paralyzed by fear that they would not be able to tolerate a more "in your face" program. Journeys of Wisdom helps wounded souls move forward to self-actualization and empowerment and plants the seeds of awakening.

27
The Artist's Way

Writing has always been an outlet for me. I put pen to paper and release my feelings in a way I can never do verbally. I was never consistent with my writing, though, so instead of a long-term steady marriage, I had an intense but sporadic love affair with the pen. It was fun while it lasted, but the episodes never lasted long enough to sustain a meaningful relationship.

I needed to write as a process of self-discovery and therapy, and I needed to write to share what I had learned with others. If my story sparks even one memory, perhaps someone else won't have to spend nearly a half-century sleepwalking through life. Maybe my writing will trigger a memory in just one person so that one of their dear friends won't have to face having a skillet fly past her ear. Mostly though, because I am a writer, I need to write.

It sounds easy enough, but our left brains, our "survival brains," try hard to protect us from harm. Unfortunately for old "Lefty," anything new or different must mean danger, and so it puts up blocks like little log jams to prevent the creative energy from flowing freely. Typically, I would allow little pieces from my creative side to trickle around the edges of the log jam. At times the little pieces were very creative, interesting to read, but they never dug deep, and they were never consistent in their arrival. I might write intensely for several days and then not return to it for weeks or even months.

Ian, who was a talented artist in this life, knew the value writing held for my human emotional healing. Persistent while he was in his earthwalk, he is relentless from the other side. Joerdie would call me with messages from Ian like, "It's time to stop being a clever arranger of words, and begin writing from your soul." To write more would mean to step outside my comfort zone into uncharted territory, to dig deeper into my past in order to rescue and recover my truth. It might also force me to shed my victim energy. I was terrified by the prospect, but neither Joerdie nor Ian are content to maintain the status quo. If the pot needs to be stirred, one of them will gladly stir it. In the case of Ian, he uses what he fondly refers to as the "hot poker up the butt" approach. He'll wake me from a sound sleep and not leave me alone until I get out of bed and write. It will feel like the message is burning a hole in my head in an effort to get out. In fact, when I wrote an uncharacteristically dark poem for a creative writing class, I tried to attribute it to Ian. His response was: "Hey, it's not me. I'm the hot-poker-up-the-butt man to get you writing, not the writer! You might check with Dorothy Parker. She's not so busy."

I learned to ignore even Ian's "subtle" approach. I would lie in bed, sometimes for hours, wide awake, silently screaming at Ian, "Go away and leave me alone!" Sometimes I would bargain with him. "Just let me sleep uninterrupted until 6 a.m., and I will get up and write for three hours." When 6 a.m. rolled around, he would wake me. I would still refuse to get up and write.

I was so terrified of writing my story that even if I sat down at my desk, I would soon be playing computer solitaire, checking my email, balancing my checkbook, anything except writing. Eventually, exhausted from my avoidance ploys, I would take a nap, the biggest avoidance ploy of all. Joerdie would periodically call to see if I was writing, and because I wasn't, I slipped back into my old pattern of victim mode, feeling ashamed by my lack of discipline.

Then, as it loves to do, the Universe intervened. In a delightful bit of synchronicity, on an airplane, Joerdie met and struck up a conversation with a total stranger who happened to be a writer. For no apparent reason, this unknown woman went on to tell Joerdie that she had been blocked as a writer for a number of years before she discovered a book that had changed her life and her writing. The book was *The Artist's Way* by Julia Cameron. The Universe frequently uses Joerdie as a vessel for passing along information or connecting people who need to meet, because Joerdie is open to new experiences and has learned to listen. If I had encountered this same stranger, I would have said a quick "hello" before averting my eyes to discourage any further contact.

When Joerdie told me about *The Artist's Way*, I immediately bought it, somewhat surprised to find it at the small bookstore in Lima, Ohio. The Universe, as always, provided everything I needed; true to character, I did my best to ignore the signs it was sending my way. I was comfortable being a victim. I promptly added the book to my extensive collection of metaphysical books that I had never read—filed alphabetically by author and logged into my database entitled "Book Inventory." (Organizing the smallest anal detail of my life was also a favorite ploy to avoid writing.)

Several months later, tired of Ian and his hot poker, I began reading *The Artist's Way*. I was amazed by what I found. As I've discussed earlier, much of my emotional recovery work has involved helping my inner children to feel safe to reveal the past so that we can work together on healing it. It was these inner children who were present and remember the horrible human experience of the abuse my soul agreed to experience. Just as Journeys of Wisdom had done earlier, *The Artist's Way* works with inner children, allowing them to express themselves through art.

Ms. Cameron believes that creativity is the natural state of being. We are all artists in one form or another, whether we seek it as a full-time career or just a healthy emotional outlet. She also contends that our artists are children who have retreated inside because of a lack of encouragement: societal or familial judgments that artists are lazy, financially irresponsible, promiscuous, drug or alcohol addicted, or anything else that would indicate to old "Lefty" that danger is afoot and force the discouraged artist to retreat to the deep recesses of the psyche.

The Artist's Way is a twelve-week program that gently and humorously guides the reader through the fears that block their creative sides. It works with the artist inner child to dispel the myths and remove the fear. Of course, what works for the artist inner child is also effective for the other frightened, wounded inner children we carry. So while the artist within is being healed and released, so too are all the other wounded inner children. Cameron's program has been a tremendous tool in my overall spiritual journey, as well as in releasing the blocks that prevented me from writing.

The Artist's Way not only provided powerful tools for my overall recovery, but also got me writing on a regular basis. Because the program was so intense, and from the human standpoint, I was so wounded when I went through it the first time, I chose to go through the program several more times throughout my reawakening process. I found that each time I completed the work, I learned more about myself and peeled away more layers of fear that held me in victim mode.

28

The Artist's Way Creativity Camp

The material in *The Artist's Way* was so powerful that it led me to attend The Artist's Way Creativity Camp in Taos, New Mexico, which provided a major boost to move me to the next level of human emotional healing and spiritual awakening.

The Artist's Way Creativity Camp represented a major turning point in my awakening, because it was the first time I had ventured out of the comfort of my support group, namely Joerdie, Eric, Dan, and Jim, since the flashbacks began. I had gone to Journeys of Wisdom but that was in Columbus, only ninety miles away; if I was too uncomfortable, I could just drive home. It was only three days for each session. At less than $200 for each weekend program, it was also inexpensive enough that forfeiting the money would not have been an issue. By contrast, The Artist's Way was 1,500 miles away in New Mexico, the tuition substantially more, plus I had airfare, car rental, and hotel expenses, and it lasted a full week.

I was terrified. Social situations involving more than two or three close friends have always been excruciating for me. I can't begin to count the number of weddings, parties, and other social functions that I had planned to attend, only to be overcome by a debilitating panic attack at the last minute. Frequently I would be dressed and ready to walk out the door, but just couldn't bring myself to be in a social situation where I would be forced to try to make small talk with a large group of people. Fear is the basis of being a victim. Traveling across the country alone to be with a group of total strangers for a week was a major challenge for me from the human standpoint. Although most people shared double rooms, I opted to pay twice as much to have a single room—a private sanctuary into which I could retreat if necessary.

Taos is a haven for artists of all types. The camp was located at a little inn on the outskirts of town, a place conducive to any type of creative endeavor, and the camp was not limited to writers. There were painters, sculptors, photographers, even a psychologist-turned-stand-up-comedian. None of us were kids; the average age was about 40, probably indicative of a group of people ready to wake up and make changes in our lives, and finally discover who we really were. At fifty, I was near the top of the range, but it didn't matter. Most of us were just waking up, tired of sleepwalking through old lives, ready to realize our dreams through some artistic means. We were a group of like souls, nonjudgmental and totally supportive of each other. While I initially spent much of my time alone, I felt safe enough to participate in everything the camp offered, and made several lasting friendships, which was a huge step for me.

Poet James Navé, who began working with *The Artist's Way* creator Julia Cameron in 1995, was creative director of the camp. We opened each day of the camp with Qigong or yoga, followed by a morning lecture session with Ms. Cameron. She took us through writing exercises from *The Artist's Way*, designed to release any blockages that were keeping us from realizing our dreams of pursuing our art. The exercises were intense, designed to get us in touch with our feelings, and like Journeys of Wisdom, frequently forced us to come face-to-face with our inner children.

The exercise that touched me most deeply—changed my life really—was to write a short fairytale about whatever personal demon was blocking the path to our creative dream. At the end of the fairytale, we were instructed to kill our creative demon so that we would be free. While I generally ponder what I'm going to write, in this case I knew immediately. Almost as soon as Julia gave the assignment, the title popped into my head: "Princess Incestia." I told a tale of a princess and her father, King Peter the Pedophile. It was short, only two pages, and it summarized my story as I understood it at that point. I knew the minute I wrote it that it was powerful. It was the first time I had attempted to write any portion of my story, and I

believe it was possible because the format of a fairy tale made my inner children feel safe enough to let it emerge. We broke into small groups the next day and shared our stories with our groups. I couldn't complete mine without sobbing, but I did get through it. It was early in the week, and after reading my fairytale to this intimate group, I was suddenly liberated and empowered, able to really participate in the rest of the camp.

Even though the fairytale was about abuse rather than sacred contracts, it was important for me because I was finally able to acknowledge the fear with which I had lived my life up to that point. Releasing the fear was imperative to shedding the victim energy.

The daily sessions with Ms. Cameron were wonderful. She is an excellent teacher, combining quick wit with a strong sense of spirituality. She wrote the book, so there is no one who can present the concepts and material from *The Artist's Way* in a more compelling or authoritative way. The rest of the camp, however, was equally powerful in providing artistic outlets.

In the afternoons, we could choose from a variety of activities, such as songwriting with singer/songwriter Walter Parks, a Lyle Lovett look-alike with an unruly mop of dark brown hair and laid-back style, or poetry writing with Navé, who by contrast has a shaved head and is extremely intense. Other choices included fabric painting, photography, doll making, and African drumming. I tried everything once, but from the moment my hand first touched the skin of the drum, I was hooked on drumming. The vibration and rhythm resonated with me in a way that I can barely describe. It was like I had returned to some long-forgotten roots, a former African life I suspect. From that point on, I skipped every other optional activity so that I could drum.

The last night of the camp was an open mic, where anyone who wanted to could perform for the rest of the group. Up until dinner that evening, immediately before the show began, I did not plan to participate. I definitely couldn't sing or play a musical instrument. I didn't have any poetry I had written, and I certainly was not a stand-up comedian. There was nothing I could share with the group. Then I remembered my fairytale. Did I dare read it? It was so personal and possibly offensive. Not as offensive as my singing, of course, but still I wasn't sure it was appropriate. Finally I decided, "What the hell.

I'm leaving tomorrow, and I never have to see any of these people again if this doesn't go well." We had shared a lot over the previous week, and I knew that these were people I could trust.

We drew numbers to select who would go first. When I drew number two, I was greatly relieved, because I wouldn't have to wait and worry for an hour or more before my turn. My friend Laurie was first. She sang a spirited rendition of Dusty Springfield's "Son of a Preacher Man," the perfect thing to warm up the crowd for a fairy-tale about incest, I thought.

I knew that what I was about to do was a major step, probably the most important thing I had yet tried. I knew that if I was suc-cessful, it would change my life forever.

I walked to the front, nervously clutching the microphone in my sweaty palm. "I'm going to read my fairytale—The one we wrote for class," I said quietly. Disappointed sighs emanated from the audi-ence. Maybe this wasn't such a good idea. I continued. "It's called Princess Incestia." They laughed. Then I began to read, my voice cracking more with emotion than nerves.

> "Princess Incestia lived in the Kingdom of Lost Innocence with her father, King Peter the Pedophile. Incestia loved her father very much. He loved her even more."

I heard nervous laughter, and then silence as the audience grasped the gravity of what I was reading. I continued, my voice now becoming strong and clear.

> "He loved her in a way no child should ever have to remember, and so she didn't."

Now the silence from the crowd was deafening. Dead silence. I didn't know if I should continue reading, or run from the room in tears as a victim would normally choose to do. I continued.

> "As she grew older, the princess sank into a sort of dark dream—more of a nightmare really. She became distant and withdrawn because she always

felt she was different. It wasn't just that she was a princess. It was something else, something dark and terrible, but Incestia didn't know what it was. She couldn't remember the joyous days of her childhood. In fact, she could barely remember her childhood at all. Her emotions were numb, except for the cloud of sadness that always hung over her like a heavy fog. She never understood why.

"When King Peter passed over into the Netherworld, her sadness grew even more intense. Incestia could not escape the sadness. It lasted for many years.

"Then one day something wonderful happened. Princess Incestia awoke from her nightmare. The darkness left, and she began to remember. She remembered all of the unspeakable things her father had done to her—only they weren't unspeakable anymore. Princess Incestia finally found her voice and began to tell people what she remembered. At first they didn't believe her; he was the king, after all. How could she say such terrible things about her own beloved father, especially when he wasn't there to defend his honor? Incestia knew in her heart that she had finally found her truth. She continued to speak and then she began to write about her memories. She wrote so that other little princesses would hear her words, awaken from their nightmares, and begin to remember too. Perhaps she could save even one child from the terrible sadness that she had endured. As she wrote, something wonderful happened. The fog of sadness lifted, and she had a whole new life—a life filled with love and peace and joy.

"Princess Incestia—or Princess Happy Feet, as she now preferred to be called—had broken free from King Peter the Pedophile. She didn't need to kill him. His power over her was already dead."

As I finished reading, the audience, all of my new friends, rose to their feet and began to applaud wildly. People came forward from the crowd to embrace me. It was one of the threshold moments of my life. Several people said that I had told their stories, and thanked me for my courage. To me, it didn't seem courageous at all.

At breakfast the next morning, Richard, the psychologist-turned-stand-up-comedian, recounted his initial memories of the abuse he agreed to experience. He was riding the elevator in his building on his way to his office when another man got on. The man reeked of alcohol and a certain brand of aftershave that was familiar to Richard. The combination of the two scents triggered the memories of the abuse he had agreed to and the man who agreed to play his abuser. It reminded me of the book Jim had given me that had the same mildewed scent as the paperback sex novels from my dad's darkroom, and how I burst into tears when I smelled it.

Richard told me that in his research on incest, following his own memories, he discovered that a disproportionate number of artists of all types—writers, musicians, painters, whatever the art—have agreed to experience sexual abuse as children. I raised the question, why are artistic children singled out for abuse? Are they first abused, and then turn to art as a way of coping with the experience, or are these artistic children more sensitive, more vulnerable than the general population, and therefore more attractive to the souls who have agreed to be sexual predators?

We were not able to answer any of these questions because they were not the right questions. None of us understood sacred contracts. What we should have asked was why so many souls choose the combination of abuse and art for their earthwalks. The answer is that souls never agree to more than they can handle, and more advanced souls tackle more difficult lessons. The right brain is both the artistic and spiritual side of the human. Thus more advanced souls that incarnate into human bodies generally exhibit artistic ability in some form because they are by nature right-brained. Being advanced does not mean that the souls are in any way superior. That would be a human concept. Advanced simply means the souls are further along on their journeys to enlightenment.

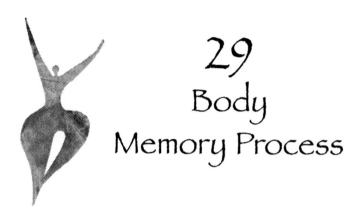

29
Body
Memory Process

I knew absolutely nothing about Body Memory Process or its creator David Sohn when Joerdie invited me to a gathering at her home to hear the psychic from Croatia channel the archangel Metatron. At that point, I had never even heard of Metatron, let alone David Sohn, but over the years I have learned to trust Joerdie.

David, it turned out, is a gifted psychic who was living in Croatia at the time, but David is decidedly American, with his George Carlin-like appearance and biting sense of humor. He did, in fact, channel Metatron that evening, but as is often the case, that was only the means of getting us together, not the purpose of our meeting.

David is trained and/or certified in a variety of healing techniques, including Neuro-Linguistic Programming, Rebirthing, Reiki, Intervention Counseling, Hypnosis, and Thai Massage, in addition to his highly developed psychic abilities. He created Body Memory Process by applying techniques from many healing paradigms. The results are astounding. The premise is that each of us has made decisions and promises throughout life which strongly influence the way we live. The most important of these decisions were made in early childhood or in the womb, so as adults we have no conscious memory of them. Dr. Deepak Chopra calls these decisions "premature cognitive commitments." When we make these decisions, they are imprinted as cellular memory and are retained as part of the energy structure of the body and eventually manifest as tension, recurrent pain, dis-ease, or negative nonworking behavior patterns. David's goal is to release this stored energy by resolving the issues that created it.

While the adults we have become can comprehend the human trauma caused by the abusive experiences to which we have agreed, it is our inner children who carry the emotional wounds. Every traumatic event that happened in our human lives is embedded in our body memory, and until those negative memories are removed and the inner child feels safe, the surviving adult will never fully heal.

David begins first with a discovery process; he helps to uncover the vows we made as infants so that they can be reviewed and reevaluated. This can be a long and excruciating process, because the information that David uncovers is generally not pleasant from the human standpoint. We tried to forget it for a reason. This is how our first session began:

"Tell me about your birth."

"I don't remember my birth. I was only a baby."

"We all have birth memories. What's the first thing you remember?"

"The old family joke is that immediately after she gave birth to me my mother asked, 'Does it look like Dr. Welby?' but I don't remember hearing that."

"Well, you did. That's the first thing you heard. Does IT look like Dr. Welby? Not she. Not the baby. Does IT look like Dr. Welby? Did your mother have an affair with Dr. Welby?"

"Yes, she admitted to me that she did. He was at our house a lot. I remember him making house calls when I was little."

"Did your father know about the affair?"

"I'm not sure. We used to joke about it, about Dr. Welby being my father."

"So the first thing your father hears after you're born is 'Does it look like Dr. Welby?' Your father was a pedophile. Here you were, this beautiful, perfect child, and you were readily available to him. You weren't his, at least as far as he knew. You were just an 'it.' The 'it' bastard of Dr. Welby."

"I always believed he was obsessed with me because of some past life we had together. Someone told me that he and I were lovers in a past life. That's why he only wanted me."

"That may be true, but you were also the perfect way for him to get revenge against your mother for having an affair with Dr. Welby. He was a pedophile. You weren't his seed. He rejected her and chose you. It couldn't have been any better for him. The reason you couldn't heal the emotional wounds from the incest is because you weren't coming at it from the right direction. You've been viewing it as excessive love when it was also revenge."

Next, the issue that created the decision is resolved, and David teaches ways for the cellular memory to unlearn the negative patterns of feelings that have been embedded there, sometimes for decades. It involves, among other things, the use of disavows to dislodge the old patterns. Similar to the affirmation process where an individual repeats affirmative statements in an effort to establish new patterns of positive feelings, disavows work to remove the old beliefs. Disavows release the old negative belief patterns that cover the wounds to our human psyche with emotional scar tissue that prevents healing and holds us in victim mode. The individual reads the disavows into a tape recorder and then plays them back, repeating them aloud twice a day for three months until the old beliefs have been released. My initial disavows included, "I disavow no one is ever going to love me like my daddy does," and "I disavow she hates me."

One of the primary components of releasing the victim energy is the willingness to forgive, which David defines as "no longer feeling the need to change the past." To facilitate forgiveness, BMP uses a tool called the Forgiveness Exercise to help the individual release the underlying anger, which in many cases has been suppressed. In the Forgiveness Exercise, the individual chooses one person per week to forgive, then every day for that week the individual will write, "I, (individual's name), completely forgive (person being forgiven)." The individual writes this sentence seventy times a day in longhand for one week, and at the end of the week he or she burns the pages, much as I did with the letters I wrote to my father and his friend following my first regression with Susan Fantz. Although it sounds simple, I found the Forgiveness Exercise to be especially powerful.

Since the exercise is designed to last for twelve weeks, I decided to start small, choose someone for whom I held relatively little anger, before advancing to the more intense people such as my parents. I began with my sister, and as expected, I felt very little emotion. The second week I chose Joerdie because despite how much we love each other, with all our karmic history, we carry a lot of emotional baggage, and again I had almost no reaction to the Forgiveness Exercise. On the third week, I chose to forgive my father. As I began writing "I, Nancy, completely forgive Leo," I felt nothing. I thought to myself, "Hey this is going to be easy." I couldn't have been more wrong. By about the tenth time on the first day that I wrote the sentence, my heart began pounding and continued intermittently for three full days. Clearly I had hit an open wound, but I persevered and wrote the sentence seventy times a day for the entire week. As intense as the first few days were, by the end of the week, I felt nothing.

The most interesting response came when I decided to forgive myself. As I began writing over and over "I, Nancy, completely forgive Nancy." I found myself frequently unable to write my own name. I would start out all right, but by the time it came to actually forgiving myself, I would write "Joerdie" or "Erica" or some other loved one.

I was so wrapped up in being a victim that I didn't believe I deserved to be forgiven, especially not by me. Part of me did not want to give up the victim role because it was comfortable. As I continued, the name issue finally being resolved, I began purging from every orifice. I was in bed and sick as a dog for three days. I kept writing though, and, as with forgiving my father, I released the negative energy. In the process I learned that forgiveness is definitely not for sissies.

Of course, from the spiritual standpoint, forgiveness is not necessary because we agreed to experience all of the behavior before beginning each earthwalk. The soul does not need to either forgive or heal. Forgiveness is to help our human hosts with their emotional wounds, and it is vitally important. Just because one knows and accepts the concept of sacred contracts does not mean he or she can immediately integrate it into the human experience.

Body Memory Therapy is not gentle, nor is it easy, but the results are amazing. David is relentless in his pursuit of the truth, because it is in knowing the truth that we can move forward. He probes and questions, forcing you to find the answers you might not want to face, peeling away layer after layer of the emotional onion. It was during my initial session with David that we realized for the first time that, from the human standpoint, my father chose me not because of some uncontrollable love but because he believed that I was not his child. I was available and acceptable to Leo since I wasn't, at least in his mind, his seed, and I was the perfect means to punish my mother for her infidelity with Dr. Welby. Of course, whatever the human behavior, it was all part of our sacred contract.

That was not a layer of the onion I was eager to remove, but it afforded me another powerful opportunity to heal. Approaching the healing from the perspective of excessive love alone was incorrect. If the premise is incorrect, the healing will be incomplete.

During my second session with David, six months after the first, I was lying on the massage table reviewing my new list of disavows with his protégé Elaine Dalyrumple. She would read the disavow; I would take a deep breath, release it, and repeat the disavow back to her. This is the same basic procedure I would use during my ninety-day healing program, except that instead of Elaine reading the disavow, I would hear my own voice recorded on a cassette tape. Noting my lack of emotion with these very intense statements, such as "I disavow, if I tell the truth, no one will ever love me," Elaine asked, "Nancy, are you in your body?"

I laughed, because, as I learned to do as a small child with my father I simply left my body to avoid anything unpleasant. Now I was using the same technique to avoid the human discomfort the disavows brought to the surface and observe what was going on from the safety of above. For the same reason it had been time for me to stop relying on Prozac and marijuana to numb my emotional pain, it was now time for me to feel the human emotions the disavows would bring forward.

Although I have been doing it my entire life, I have not always been aware of when my spirit leaves and returns to my body, nor have I had much control over it. When my human host feels threatened, it just happens. I am only now developing the ability to control the phenomenon. Elaine continued to try to urge me to come back, and I would laugh, not really knowing what to do, and say, "But I'm obviously somewhere in the same room; isn't that good enough?"

Elaine, who is a Reiki practitioner, would place her hands on my feet and other parts of my body in an effort to ground me, but no matter what she tried, as soon as she read one of the disavows with which I was uncomfortable, my spirit would pop right out again.

Finally, frustrated and confused, Elaine declared that she was going to "go get David." We both laughed because it was akin to being sent to the principal's office for misbehaving. She returned with David, and they both worked with my body's energy to try to keep me present.

As Elaine read each disavow, David would ask me what kind of body sensation I was having. If I wasn't in the body, I wasn't feeling anything. One time I had a shooting sensation up my neck, another time my entire body vibrated from the intensity of the human emotion the statement evoked. Finally as Elaine read my last disavow, "I disavow I have to let him love me," keeping in mind that my inner child equated abuse with love, David leaned over and whispered in my ear. "Or I will kill your kitties." I immediately burst into tears, sobbing violently as I released all those years of buried human pain. There was no question that I was in my body or that my human host was feeling the emotion.

30
Holographic Repatterning

As with almost anything new I try, at least in the metaphysical realm, I learned about Holographic Repatterning through Joerdie. She put me in contact with Marie Fairchild of Apple Lakes Nutrition who, in addition to being an HR Practitioner, is also a Certified Nutritionist. Although we have been working together for several years, I have never met Marie in person. All of our work together has been by telephone from her office in Hercules, California, so during an early appointment when she instructed me to hold the Jin Shin point with my ring finger, I thought she might be toying with me. She was not. HR, it turns out is a powerful healing modality that makes it possible for us to create positive change in any area of our lives where we experience limitation.

Holographic Repatterning was developed by Chloe Faith Wordsworth by studying a variety of healing systems including her personal training in Acupuncture, Polarity Therapy, and brain integration. She combined this training with her knowledge of psychology, physics, holograms, and sound frequencies to create this system of self-healing. She also incorporates ancient knowledge of the Chakra system of India and the Five Element-Meridian system of China. She includes numerous modalities for creating coherence that include sound, light, movement, energetic contact, breath, and fragrance.

Coherence is a positive. It involves being connected, and holds things and people together. It allows for cohesiveness, consistency, integration, harmony, and unity. Our level of coherence determines the level of our health as well as the harmony of our relationships and the success and pleasure we receive from our life and work. Just as with everything on Classroom Earth, a higher level of coherence is a choice. It enables us to choose how to respond to life circumstances and people. We can react and move to a lower level of vibratory frequency into non-coherence, or we can respond in such a way that we move to a higher level of vibratory frequency into coherence, understanding, and love. We can choose love or we can choose fear.

Non-coherence is negative and always involves disintegration, disharmony, incongruity, incompatibility, extinction, and death. Sickness, pain, upsets in relationships, problems in our work: all involve some level of non-coherence. When we are in a non-coherent phase, we feel controlled and overwhelmed by life circumstances and people. Our tendency when non-coherent is always to react from our own outdated, non-coherent patterns. We fall back into victim mode.

Understanding that we are a pulsing field of energy or frequency opens the possibility for change: thoughts, feelings, and problems are all frequencies, and frequencies can be brought into phase with what is coherent. The HR Process gives us the means to identify those frequencies that are non-coherent and to bring them into phase with life-enhancing frequencies. Thus, problems simply let us know that we have areas of non-coherence that need to be identified and transformed with positive change.

Positive change is always experienced on three levels. It involves a new learning or new awareness known as learning coherence in HR. This awareness enables us to change on the personal level, to change how we are and who we are. This is called personal coherence. Learning and personal coherence make it possible for us to move to a higher frequency level in our relationships. This is known as relationship coherence. This triad forms a tetrahedron: learning coherence, personal coherence, and relationship coherence. The point at the apex of the tetrahedron, where all the lines of the process meet, is the point of integration. This integration occurs when our awareness and personal and relationship frequencies are in phase with coherence.

In the old paradigm of Newtonian physics, life is a machine that either quickly or slowly stagnates, winds down, disintegrates, and finally becomes extinct. This is the law of entrophy. From the Newtonian perspective, negative change as deterioration is inevitable.

In the new paradigm of Chaos theory, although change may be inevitable, non-coherence is optional. The new physics perspective on change is that we have the potential to move to higher levels of coherence, order, and awareness. By constantly making use of the window of opportunity that our problems offer us, we are able to recreate ourselves out of the chaos of our life experiences at higher levels of coherence and consciousness. In addition, this law states that there is an infinite hierarchy of order, harmony, and coherence that we have the potential to realize.

Positive change is a limitless process of growth to higher levels of awareness. At each new point of growth there is apparent chaos or problems and challenges to be faced, out of which new possibilities for continued growth emerge. With this perspective, problems are welcomed as a means for identifying and transforming outdated attitudes so we can move to higher levels of coherence and positive change. While Wordsworth doesn't specifically mention sacred contracts, she nonetheless understands how the Universe presents opportunities for our spiritual growth.

Because all our appointments are via telephone, I don't know precisely what Marie is doing at the other end of our conversations. She begins with questions and uses muscle testing techniques to determine in what areas I might be in non-coherence. Since HR utilizes a variety of modalities, she sometimes requests that I hum a particular tone or visualize a specific color. Homework assignments are always part of the HR process, to be completed between appointments. One assignment was to purchase two plastic bottles, one blue and one yellow which I was to fill with water, and place in the sunlight for several hours. After that I was instructed to wash my eyes out with the water. Another time I was to buy specific essential oils, and bathe in them three times a week for six weeks. When I commented that I thought that was a rather odd assignment, Marie laughed and said, "It's not that odd. Sometimes the book says the client has to take singing lessons."

While Wordsworth emphasizes that Holographic Repatterning is not a spiritual path or a religion, it is a powerful tool for replacing negative lower vibrational behavior and perceptions caused by fear with the coherence that represents love and light.

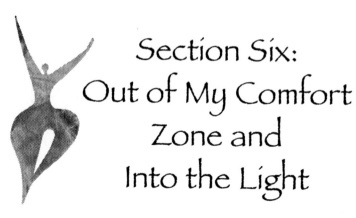

Section Six:
Out of My Comfort
Zone and
Into the Light

31
Crazymakers and Other Unnecessary Clutter

I knew I had reached a new level in releasing the victim energy when I began to eliminate possessions and relationships from my life that no longer represented who I was or where I was going on my spiritual path.

The purge began slowly and innocently enough with a bathroom drawer. I cast all the cosmetic samples and make-up mistakes into the trash. I chuckled when I pitched the red shampoo from my carrot top days, remembering how my mother had begged me not to stop dying my hair. Out went the blades from razors lost years before, dried up shoe polish, and old shower caps "borrowed" from hotels.

Then the purge spread from drawer to drawer, closet to closet. Things slowly began disappearing. It was like watching a cancer being cured as I began reclaiming parts of my space. It represented my emotional healing, but it was by no means painless. On the first pass through, for every item I removed, at least three more remained. Some items were removed and replaced two or three times before they took their final bow. While I was pleased with the progress, it pained me to part with anything. I tried desperately to pass things off to my friends. Surely someone could use a bag of perfectly good shoulder pads. When my friend opened a second-hand store downtown, we joked that she initially stocked it in large part with the things I had forced her to take home. There were things even she wouldn't take, and I reluctantly pitched them.

I gave Aunt Emma's old wing-backed chairs to my cousin who

was building a new house. The chairs were especially important because they were a source of friction between my mother and me. She didn't want them for herself, but she didn't like that I had them, and while I had no particular emotional attachment to them, I kept them to annoy her. It was just part of our game. Now I was finally willing to release them and the negative energy they held in my life.

Since cooking never really caught on with me, I sold my huge antique dining room furniture, including the table with enough leaves to accommodate a NATO summit, to my friend Janet, and replaced it with a simple glass-top table, far more appropriate for tacos or the occasional salmon casserole.

"You're going to miss that big buffet with all that storage space for your good china," my mother cautioned.

"No, Mother," I told her. "I'm going to be just fine." I didn't have the heart to tell her that I wouldn't need the buffet because the china, too, was gone. I even disposed of my extensive cat collection with felines of every description including the little wooden ones with the ears chewed off by a jealous dog. Nothing was sacred.

The most significant moment came when I gave away the blouse I was wearing when my father passed over, an oversized silk shirt with large, Garth Brooks-type patches of green, orange, yellow, and blue on the front. It was solid black in the back, and I always loved that blouse. Although I never wore it again, I kept it for seven years, even taking it with me when we moved. It had served as a solemn reminder of my terrible loss and now it represented the victim energy that I was ready to release. Even when I realized that I no longer needed it, I still left it folded neatly in plain view for several weeks before I finally had the courage to remove it permanently from the house.

Gone were the hideous striped knit shirt and plaid polyester pants that my dad always wore when he came for breakfast. The only things I kept were the cards he sent me over the years, the agate ring, and the tap shoes, and even those treasures ended up packed away in a box, no longer on display.

In the closets, I found clothing in every size. If it didn't fit at that moment, out it went. That included the only size four dress I ever owned. I never thought I would part with that; it certainly didn't take up much space. And why, I wondered as I emptied boxes into the trash, did I ever think I would want to go back and revisit old underwear I had worn as a teenager?

I went through boxes of Erica's old school papers. From nursery school until about fifth grade when she learned to adequately forge my signature and thus never needed to bring anything else home, I had saved every single paper she had ever created. For each year there was a box, and each box was filled to the rim with sheet after sheet of stick figures, spelling lists, and math papers; anything she had touched, I had saved. At least some of it had to go. I carefully sorted through each box and saved a representative sampling of her creative genius. I saved the sign I found tacked to the old maple tree in front of our house when she was about five. "CAT 4 SALE" it read. She had found the solution for ridding the house of my beloved Lee Ann, Erica's rival for my affection.

The purge extended to relationships that no longer worked. Part of being a victim was surrounding myself with other victims whom I allowed to drain my time and energy so I could complain about how put upon I was. I call them the crazymakers because they invariably swooped down in full crisis mode at the least opportune times.

They flocked to me, of course, because I was their queen. We had a mutually satisfying co-dependent relationship based on who could create the biggest drama with the most colossal crisis. Most of the time we weren't looking for solutions. We were only caught up in the crisis and the attention and adrenaline rush it brought us. We were all fulfilling our commitments to the victim roles we agreed to play with each other.

As I began to step out of the victim energy, the relationships no longer worked for any of us and they drifted out of my life.

While I can happily report that I no longer attract the crazy-makers or hang onto emotional clutter, the same is not always true of the physical clutter in my life. Whenever piles and boxes of really important stuff that I haven't touched for months begin to fill my house, I call my wonderful but totally ruthless friend Shirley Jacquay. She will arrive with boxes and trash bags and before I know it, my treasures have gone either to charity or the dumpster. When she leaves, my home is once again peaceful and clutter-free. Shirley has no use for either crazymakers or clutter of any kind.

32
When Failing Is the
Ultimate Success

As part of my quest for knowledge and self-discovery, I periodically take classes at Antioch College, an extremely freethinking liberal arts college in Yellow Springs, Ohio, which I chose specifically because it is so liberal and so entirely different from anything I would ever encounter in my "normal" life. The fall semester 2002 began as I was midway through the first draft of this book, and I seriously debated whether I should take even one class or instead concentrate all my energy on writing. When Joerdie checked with spirit, it indicated I was going to learn an important lesson beyond what was offered in the classroom.

I registered for Introduction to Africana Studies. Being from Wapakoneta, a small town where the only diversity, besides a small influx of Southeast Asians in the early '80s, was the Catholics or Democrats, I thought it would be interesting. I had already taken a powerful Women's Studies class. Africana Studies seemed like the next logical progression in my quest for knowledge.

My instructor was an intense young man originally from Guyana named Jahwara Giddings. I'm sure he had never encountered a student like me in his short teaching career. I was older than the parents of most of his other students, and my opinions were slightly to the left of anyone named Kennedy.

After the first class, when I saw the syllabus and heard what Jahwara expected from each of us, I immediately scheduled a conference with him to discuss whether, in light of the fact that I was in the throes of writing a book, I should merely audit the class. I still had a touch of the crazymaker drama queen, victim in me. To audit, I would not be required to do any of the work, but could still participate as much as I wanted. The downside would be that I would never be permitted to take the class for credit once I had audited it, and without the pressure of possibly failing, the likelihood of my reading all of the material and thus learning as much as I would by taking the class for credit was small. Jahwara was encouraging; I decided to take the course for credit and do my best to keep up.

Within a week, I knew I was in trouble. I was already behind in the papers I was required to write, but I convinced Jahwara that with a small extension I could catch up and remain current. I believed it at the time. The next week I was attending a writing retreat in Sedona, Arizona, so in order not to miss any classes, I scheduled my flights so that I would leave after class on Wednesday and return late Sunday night. We were only permitted to miss two classes total; I didn't want to waste one of my absences so early in the semester. I had three short papers due for class on Monday, but I figured I could get them written in my "free" time in Sedona and type them when I got home at midnight on Sunday. I knew it wasn't reasonable, but I also knew that I had never failed a class, and I wasn't willing to start at that point in my life.

The Universe was about to teach me a lesson that I didn't want to learn. When I tried to print something Tuesday night, I discovered my printer was not working. I called Steve, my computer guru friend, for advice and tried everything he suggested. Still no printer. I was leaving directly from class Wednesday; I wouldn't be back until after midnight Sunday. Class was at 8:30 Monday morning. I was in crazymaker trouble. On my way out the door after class I explained the situation briefly to Jahwara. He suggested that I write the papers as neatly as possible in longhand. I'm left-handed, with large, sprawling handwriting. Besides being illegible, three papers in longhand would take forever to write (plus I hadn't read the material I was to write about).

I left for Sedona preoccupied with my papers and how I could possibly complete them on time. I finally decided that if I could find a Kinkos in Sedona, I could type and print the papers there. Of course, there was not a Kinkos or anything like it in Sedona, a small artsy town filled with writers, painters, sculptors, and psychics who were also writers, painters, and sculptors. They didn't need a Kinkos. Why was I surprised? I should have recognized the moment the printer failed that the Universe was at work.

The writing retreat was at the house of my mentor Tom Bird; after I explained my situation, he offered to let me use his computer and printer. Problem solved. Not quite. I still had to read two long chapters before I could begin to write the papers, and it was taking forever. Trying to concentrate on the retreat work and my reading assignments, I was having trouble doing either. I was becoming frustrated and irritable. Finally, on Saturday afternoon, I finished the reading and drove back to Tom's house to type the papers, while everyone else from the retreat was on a hike in Sedona's famous red rocks. Everyone that is, except the one guy who was using the computer "for a few minutes"; an hour and a half later he was still on the computer. I was in a panic. Normally I would have just explained the situation to him and then, if necessary, physically removed him from the chair. The Universe, however, was trying to teach me a valuable lesson.

Instead of talking to this perfectly reasonable man, I stormed out and drove back to my rented house to regroup. What could I do? There was no Kinkos in Sedona, but there was one about fifteen miles from my apartment in Yellow Springs. Of course, it was small, not one of the open-all-night kinds. I decided that I could stay up all night Sunday typing the papers, drive to Kinkos to be waiting outside when it opened at 7 a.m., print the papers, and rush back to Yellow Springs for my 8:30 class. It was a ridiculous plan that probably wouldn't have worked when I was twenty, let alone in my fifties. I'm usually in bed before 11:00 o'clock. It's been years since I've seen the ball drop in Times Square on New Year's, and I doubted I was capable of pulling an all-nighter. I was in full-blown crazymaker mode.

I was suddenly struck by how ridiculously I was behaving, just so that I could pass a class. It was another of those major "Aha" moments in my life as I became aware that the Universe was throwing all of those obstacles in my path so that I would stop and reevaluate my priorities. The lesson was about far more than just these particular papers. It was about letting go of the need to be perfect, something I had never done. Yet I knew now that I had to give myself the option of failing the class while at the same time being at peace with the decision. It sounds easy enough, but it wasn't.

I called Erica, because she has a knack for cutting right to the core of an issue. She can be ruthless. Dan and I still laugh about the summer program she attended at the University of Colorado in Boulder when she was in high school. The students in her group decided that a particular instructor was being unreasonable, and elected Erica to talk to the woman because she was the "most diplomatic." We shuddered to think what the rest of the class must have been like to select Erica because of her diplomacy!

"I can't get all my work done, Erica. I'm either going to have to drop the class or fail it," I sobbed.

"So fail it," she responded with such cavalier calm that I forgot for a moment why I was so upset. "It's no big deal. You can always take it again later. Mom, you're over fifty and you only take one class at a time. At that rate, it's not like you're going to be getting a degree in the next twenty years anyway. The book is much more important than one class."

"But you don't understand. I've never failed anything before. I don't know if I can handle it."

"Well, it's time you find out, isn't it? Maybe you can just withdraw, and it will be like you never took the class. You might even get some money back."

"I think it's too late to withdraw. I think I'm going to have to fail."

"So then fail. I'm telling you, it's not a big deal."

She was right. It should not be a big deal. I was beginning to embrace the idea that it was not disgraceful to fail. Disgraceful to whom I wondered?

That being said, I called Dan. "I can't get all the work done and I've decided to fail the class."

"OK."

"What do you mean, OK? I'm going to forfeit all that money and I'm going to fail the class, and all you can say is OK?" Crazymakers hate rational thinking.

"It's no big deal. Get what you can out of the class just for the joy of learning, and don't worry about failing. It doesn't matter. The book is more important."

"You mean it doesn't matter if I fail?"

"It doesn't matter if you fail."

One might expect that I would be feeling much better by this time. I knew in my heart that surrendering and allowing myself the experience of failing, if that was to be the outcome, was my lesson to learn. Yet my stubborn, left-brain ego kept screaming.

Before I realized each earthwalk is a game with no winners or losers, only participants, I was unbelievably competitive. I would do almost anything to win. Joerdie still talks about when her boys were small, probably three and five; I would play Candyland with them, and not only didn't I let them win, as most adults would have done, I wouldn't let them stop playing until I won! Joerdie said they would be almost in tears, begging me to let them go to bed.

When I would argue, or more likely pout, they would try their best to throw the game in my favor, which was virtually impossible because it was a very simple board game. At three and five, these sweet little boys were behaving far more maturely than I was. They finally refused to play with me anymore!

Ironically, all weekend at the retreat I had been writing about facing fear. The Universe had presented me with several major tests in recent days that I sailed through with no difficulty. As I wrote about each one, I talked about how once we face our fears they no longer hold power over us, and they usually turn out to be much less traumatic than we anticipated. I knew what I wrote was true, but apparently all that talk of facing fear brought other old issues to the surface. Perhaps the Universe decided that I was ready for an even bigger challenge. Whatever the cause, by the time I called Joerdie, I was a mess.

"I'm having a rough day. I have to either drop my class or fail it. I just can't get all the work done and still work on the book. I'm pretty upset. I've never failed anything before. I could just drop the class, but I really do enjoy it. I just can't get everything done."

I told her about all the walls I kept running into trying to get the papers written.

"Sounds like the Universe is making it pretty clear that you're not supposed to get them done. You need to honor that. What's your purpose in taking the class? Are you after the credit or what you can learn?"

"I'm mostly interested in learning as much as I can. It's not like I'm actively pursuing a degree. I'm just taking things that interest me. I really like this class. I don't want to drop it."

"That's your answer. The Universe is presenting you with the opportunity to be part of the experience where there is a real possibility of failure. You have to decide whether you're willing to step into that experience knowing that there is no failure. Even if you don't pass the class, you will have succeeded in allowing yourself to experience failure. You will have learned the lesson the Universe is providing, which means you didn't fail."

"I probably have the option to withdraw from the class, but if I do that it's like quitting. I would just be running away from the lesson. I'm going to stay in knowing that I'm going to fail."

"Then do it."

Not only didn't I make any heroic efforts to get the papers done, I skipped class on Monday. It was incredibly liberating, like the first time in the '60s that I discovered I would not be arrested for not wearing a bra, or when as an overweight middle-aged woman, I found that the doctor really cannot force you to step onto the scale to be weighed.

I stopped to see Jahwara later that day.

"Did I know you were going to miss class today? Was your plane late?" he began. "How about your journal papers? Can you still exchange them with someone in the class for comment before I see them?"

"I decided to sleep in this morning, and I didn't do the papers. I'm not going to pass the class."

"You're dropping out? Oh, I'm sorry. You add a lot to the class."

"I'm not dropping out; I'm just not going to pass. I don't have time to do the work, but I really enjoy the class, so I'm just going to come and glean what I can."

"Oh, so you're just going to audit?" he asked, clearly not grasping the concept of intentionally failing a class.

"No, Jahwara, I'm still going to be in the class, but I don't have time to do the work. I'm just not going to pass."

"I don't understand. Why would you do that?"

"I've always had a tremendous fear of failure, and it's time I faced it. In the past, I would have done anything to pass a class, but now it's time I allow my spirit the experience of failing. If I can allow myself to do that, it will be a tremendous lesson for me. So you see, either way I can't lose. I really like the class, so I'm going to continue to attend, and I'll do as much of the work as I have time for. The rest I'm not going to worry about."

"Well, then maybe you'll still pass the course," he said optimistically.

Jahwara, while having a great sense of humor, is serious and results-oriented when it comes to his work. He is demanding of himself as well as his students. Anything less than a best effort is totally foreign to his nature, but he was trying hard to understand why I was doing this.

"If I don't do the work, I won't pass the class. I know you don't understand why I'm doing this, rather than just dropping out and retaking the class later. Believe me, this is incredibly hard for me. I've never failed at anything in my life. Either I was excellent, or I quit before I failed. This time I'm going to honor my spirit and allow it to have the opportunity to fail."

"OK then. I guess I'll either see you or not see you in class, whatever the case may be."

He didn't fully comprehend why I was willing to fail, but he was trying hard to be supportive. For the remainder of the semester, I came to class when I could and did as much of the work as time allowed. For the first time in my life I didn't worry about being the best or having my work compared to someone else's. I was there for the pure joy of learning with no concern for the final outcome. It didn't matter.

That is not to say that "failing" came easily or naturally to me. There were times, having not done the assigned readings, that I felt extremely anxious at not being able to join in the class discussions. My ego still struggled with the notion that my worth was determined by how smart I appeared to the rest of the class. I still wanted to prove myself.

At times I felt threatened by my beautiful young classmate who knew all the answers and tended to dominate most class discussions. This young woman was extremely bright, very intense, and apparently immune to the effects of an 8:30 a.m. Monday class that rendered most of the students mute. She was the type of student every instructor prays to have in class and the type every insecure student hates to be around–especially if that insecure student happens to be a middle-aged-minivan driving wife and mother bent on failing the class. I still felt the desire to compete, even though I knew I didn't need to. It wasn't on just an intellectual level that I wanted to compete. I wanted to be the young, pretty, smart one that the other girls envied. Instead I found myself as the old, chubby one, the one who would never get a date, the one who didn't necessarily understand what was going on in the discussions. One day I raised my hand to join in the discussion with a point I felt was especially brilliant. The young woman kept talking and kept talking and then her equally handsome, bright, intense male counterpart joined in, debating back and forth with her. After about ten minutes Jahwara finally acknowledged me, saying, "Nancy, did you have your hand up a while ago?"

Rather than state my point, which seemed ridiculous compared with the intense, thoughtful responses of the left-wing Ken and Barbie, I snapped back, "That was a long time ago. Apparently it wasn't important." As it frequently does when I slip back into victim mode, my response surprised me. There I was, right back in high school, angry at what was being done "to me." Actually, my response was more controlled than my inner teenagers would have preferred. My troubled inner teens wanted to stomp out of class in a huff, an act that would have been immature in an eighteen-year old and absurd in a middle-aged woman.

The incident brought home to me just how daunting this lesson of allowing myself to fail truly was. I found the act of surrendering to be far more difficult than I had ever imagined.

About halfway through the semester, I had already missed my two allotted classes and knew I would have to miss two more classes because of another writing retreat in Sedona. I emailed Jahwara.

"I've already missed the two classes I am allowed to miss, and I have to miss two more. Will I automatically fail the class? My real question is do I need to bother studying for the midterm? I'm not asking for special treatment. This is just a straight up yes or no question."

Jahwara responded, "I thought you didn't care about failing. Why don't you just relax and enjoy the ride?"

I laughed out loud as I read his response. Despite his initial reluctance, Jahwara now fully understood and accepted what I was trying to do, and was gently prodding me to follow my path. I wrote back and thanked him for helping me stay on course.

I did not receive credit for the class; in fact, I didn't even take the midterm or complete my class project. In the end I felt what could almost be described as elation. By allowing my soul to experience human failure, I learned a more important lesson on Classroom Earth.

33
Peace
and Transition

Despite our rocky beginning, over the years Dan's mother and I developed a close friendship. I was never going to be a homemaker, at least not as defined by her high standards, but my stock improved dramatically when Erica was born. There may have been dead flies in my windowsills, but at least I was a good mother.

A smart, witty woman, Janet prided herself on being able to complete the New York Times crossword puzzles in ink. When around 1988 she began displaying the early signs of Alzheimer's disease, losing words and forgetting things, Lucas took her to every medical expert he could find, including those at the Mayo and Cleveland Clinics. She had experimental surgery but nothing seemed to slow the progress of the devastating dis-ease she had chosen to experience. At first she was able to compensate for losing specific nouns by calling them "things" and going into more elaborate descriptions of their functions, but little by little, she was losing her ability to speak and her ability to care for herself.

It was during this time that Janet and I forged our special bond. As she lost her ability to speak, people who encountered her frequently assumed she also had no comprehension, which couldn't have been further from the truth. They would be extremely condescending at times, speaking about her as though she weren't there. Of course, they were only playing their roles in her drama, but at the time, it was frustrating for her, and it didn't sit well with me either.

For many years she was the patient of a neurologist who agreed to be particularly arrogant in this earthwalk. When I took her for a routine visit shortly before he retired, he ignored her completely and directed all his questions to me. I could see she was frustrated and upset.

Finally I said, "Look, don't treat Janet as though she isn't here. She may not be able to respond verbally to your questions, but she knows exactly what you're saying. If you have a question, ask her first, and if she can't answer it, I'll be happy to help."

The doctor played his part well. He sneered and responded, "Oh, so she knows what's going on, huh? Well, what day is it, Janet? Who is the President of the United States, Janet? What year is it, Janet?"

"Of course she can't answer those questions. She has no need to know any of that anymore." I didn't understand sacred contracts. I only knew that he was insulting a woman I loved.

With that bit of encouragement, Janet straightened in her chair, looked the arrogant doctor in the eye, and in her best "You're the dumbest thing I've ever seen" voice said clearly, but haltingly, "Why....should....I?"

Why should she try to remember insignificant facts that had no relevance to her life? She was struggling just to survive. It was a great moment for her—for both of us really. With three halting words, Janet had leveled this egotistical doctor, and at the same time recaptured just a bit of her dignity. The doctor stormed out of the room. Janet and I went to lunch still giggling about her accomplishment.

I found that Janet chose a particularly interesting journey this earthwalk. Most of her life she was outspoken, almost haughty, and had very little regard for anyone she considered to be incompetent, yet she chose to experience a debilitating dis-ease that would render her helpless in human terms. To make the game more intriguing, as her human condition deteriorated, she bonded with one of the humans she previously found to be the most incompetent. The family always teased me that she really didn't start to appreciate me until she lost her mind. They were, of course, correct. The further she drifted from that left logical brain and the human ego, the closer she came to her own divinity. She was able to let her own light shine, and to recognize the light in others.

Janet stayed in her own home with round-the-clock caregivers for more than a year after Lucas passed over in 1995. When she broke her hip, she had to move to a nursing home in nearby Cridersville. Though her hip healed well, the progression of the Alzheimer's dis-ease prevented her from remembering the mechanics of walking. No longer ambulatory, there was no way to bring her back to her home with its many stairs.

Even after she totally lost her ability to speak, Janet was able to communicate with her caregivers and family with her big smile and expressive eyes. I'll always remember one of the last things I heard her say. Janet nudged the woman next to her, pointed in my direction and said, "Her. Wonderful." Over the years I had apparently redeemed myself from the unfortunate mayonnaise incident.

Dan and I were delighted when her roommate at the nursing home told us one day, "You know, when she's asleep, she giggles." We knew then that during the dream time, when she was not hindered by that frail little body or the ravages of the Alzheimer's she chose to experience, Janet was probably out golfing with Lucas or sitting on the screened-in porch in Michigan, enjoying the lake.

Janet passed over with Dan and me on either side of her, each holding a hand. She opened her eyes, looked at us, and smiled. Then she closed her eyes and simply stopped breathing.

34
Driving Miss Mary

In the months following the stroke it was apparent to everyone who knew Mother that she should not be driving. Never a good driver, since the stroke her driving had only gotten worse because she no longer had the mental capacity to compensate for her lack of skill. Her friends had begun calling me to report her sometimes bizarre behavior and to say that they were afraid to ride with her anymore. My friends called to tell me that they saw her driving—not stopping or even slowing down, but merely driving, maintaining a constant speed of about twenty miles per hour through traffic lights and stop signs.

When Mother got confused, she would sometimes head in the wrong direction. She would go north when she intended to go south and would frequently end up in the wrong town. Our little home-town of Wapakoneta is surrounded by a series of even smaller communities, so there wasn't a great deal of trouble she could get into heading to one of them by mistake.

The problem became critical when she began dozing off on the sofa with her clothes on. When she would awaken and find that she was dressed, she would be frightened and confused, not knowing if it was day or night. She would call me at all hours.

"I just woke up, and I don't know what time it is."

"Well, Mother, just look at the numbers of the clock, and they will tell you," I said as gently as I could, trying to spare her feelings and her dignity.

"But is it today or tomorrow? I don't know how long I was asleep and I don't know if it is morning or night. How do I tell?"

"You can look out the window. If it's dark, then it's night, and if it's light, then it's day."

"Well, it's dark, but is it today or tomorrow?"

"It's tomorrow, Mother. Put your nightgown on and go to bed."

Sometimes that would satisfy her, but at other times, lonely and confused, she would get in her car and try to drive to her ex-husband's house in Sidney twenty miles away down Interstate 75. Clogged with heavy semi-truck traffic, it was far too dangerous for a befuddled, elderly woman to be driving on. When she drove to Sidney late one night in an ice storm, I knew it was time to act for her own safety.

Peggy and I shared power of attorney after the first stroke, but because I lived in the same town as Mother, I tried to take care of the day-to-day situations that arose. I called her doctor and explained Mother's behavior. He agreed that she needed to be evaluated and said that he would send her for a driving test. At her next regular appointment, he broached the subject gently.

"Mary, are you still driving?"

"Yes."

"You know, Mary, after a stroke like the one you've had, sometimes there's a problem with the part of the brain that controls driving, so I think we better get you tested. Do you understand?"

"Yes."

He ordered a test at the local hospital using a simulator, to be followed, if necessary, by an in-car driving test.

On the way home from the doctor's office, Mother turned to me and said, "What did he say about me driving?"

"He said you need to take a test to be sure it's safe for you to drive. Whenever you want to take the test, let me know, and I'll go with you."

She was silent, but I could almost hear the wheels turning. The ability to drive represented her freedom. Mother chose a life as a fiercely independent woman to the point of recalcitrance, and it was obvious she wasn't going to give up driving without a fight.

She never called me about taking her for the simulated test, but a week or so later a technician from the hospital called me.

"Your mother and her husband were here for her driving test. They wandered all around the hospital confused, not knowing where to go. Personally, I don't think either one of them should be allowed on the road, but your mother is the only one we're concerned with at this point.

"Mrs. Fischer, we gave your mother a full range of tests in the simulator including reflex time, comprehension, and maneuverability. The only thing she passed was the vision test."

My mother had cataracts. If vision was her strong suit, what must have the rest of her skills been like?

"Anyway, Mrs. Fischer, I ordered an in-car driving test with one of our examiners, and she didn't pass any of it. She ran stop signs. She turned left from the right lane when she was supposed to turn right. Mrs. Fischer, your mother has no business being behind the wheel of a car."

My heart sank. I already knew she shouldn't be driving, but I also knew what it would be like trying to get her to stop.

When as a young girl she took her driving exam for the first time, she arrived for the test alone.

"Miss Speidel, how did you get here?" the examiner asked.

"I drove."

"Alone?"

"Yes."

"Well, if you don't pass your exam, how are you going to get home?"

"I'm going to drive."

Fortunately, she passed the test, but now it was a totally different situation. The ability to drive represented the ability to maintain her lifestyle, even the ability to continue living independently in her own home.

"So what is the next step?" I asked the hospital worker. "I certainly don't want to be the one to tell her she can't drive."

"Oh, no, her doctor has a copy of the report. Doctors have to do this sort of thing all the time. They know how to handle it. He'll tell her at her next appointment, and then he's obligated to notify the Bureau of Motor Vehicles, which will order her to take a driving test. If she doesn't pass the driving test, as I'm certain she won't, she will have to surrender her license. You don't have to worry about it. It's out of your hands."

Greatly relieved, I called Peggy with the report. "We need a plan for when she loses her license so she can still get where she wants to go," I said. "She's going to be really angry, and I'm not doing this by myself. This is as much your responsibility as mine."

As soon as the words came out of my mouth, I probably should have realized that the Universe was about to give me a test. My sacred contract with Peggy had always been that she would be passive and allow me to take the blame for any situation. We both got to be victims, me for being blamed for something that wasn't my responsibility, and her for incurring my wrath. I missed the red flag the Universe was waving in my face and proceeded with my plan.

Mother already had one part-time helper whose primary responsibility was to ensure that she got to where she was supposed to be at approximately the right time. Mother belonged to several bridge groups and prior to her helper, some of them had begun to exclude Mother because she was becoming increasingly unreliable. They would call me to tell me that she was not showing up for games or coming so late that they had already called someone else to replace her. When Mother would arrive and find the substitute in her place, she would become angry.

"Mother, I've been getting phone calls from people telling me that you aren't showing up to play bridge when you're supposed to. They don't want to replace you, but not showing up is inconveniencing all of them. We need to get you some help with keeping your schedule straight and making sure you get where you're supposed to be."

"Who has been calling? Why didn't they just call me?" she snapped. "I don't like them going behind my back and talking about me. Who's been doing that? I want to call them and tell them what I think."

The fact that the information came from me immediately made it suspect to Mother. That's the way the game worked.

A retired reading teacher, Mother used to tutor students in her home, but they all eventually stopped coming after arriving several times for their appointments only to find my mother gone. The helper we found for Mother was excellent, and although she could not salvage the tutoring students, she did manage to get mother to her other appointments on time.

Peggy and I agreed we needed to have a crew of helpers lined up and ready to step in as soon as Mother got the news she could no longer drive. If she was still able to get anywhere she wanted to go, the transition to not driving would be much smoother. If she was able to maintain her active lifestyle without interruption, we believed she would be less likely to resist the change.

I ran an ad in local newspapers that read "Loving Helper Needed to Assist Elderly Woman." I also prepared a written agreement listing all of the things that Peggy and I had discussed about Mother's care, and mailed it to Peggy for her signature before Mother learned she was losing her license. I understood our sacred contract, and I thought a written agreement would protect me. I couldn't have been more wrong.

The response to the newspaper ad was good; I found several excellent candidates. Mother's original helper agreed to coordinate scheduling the other helpers. It was going to be a simple transition except that nothing involving my mother and me was ever simple. All we needed now was for her doctor to deliver the news to Mother, and we would be all set. Everything would go smoothly, and pigs would fly.

Peggy was coming Friday, the day after Mother's doctor appointment. Mother would have one day to absorb the news before Peggy came and we could go over the plan for a crew of helpers together. I would have to incur the initial wrath, but when Peggy arrived, she would convince Mother that the plan would work.

I was noticeably nervous at lunch before Mother's doctor appointment, because I understood at least two of the components of our sacred contract: No interaction between my mother and me would ever be easy, and no matter how many other people were involved, the total blame for any situation would fall directly on me. Those were the rules we agreed to in our sacred contract. The hospital worker's assurances that the doctor would take full responsibility did little to comfort me.

When her doctor entered the room, Mother was sitting on the end of the examining table, legs dangling over the side.

"Mary, we got the results back from your driving test. You didn't pass any of it. It says your reflexes were too slow to avoid an accident and that you couldn't maneuver to park. It showed that you ran a stop sign, and turned left from the right lane. That isn't good, Mary. We can't let you drive anymore."

"I slowed down and looked. There wasn't anything coming. I didn't have to stop." As always, as far as she was concerned, the rules didn't apply to her. "And I only crossed those lanes because I thought he said right. I didn't hit anything, did I?"

"No, but your driving is dangerous. We're afraid you're going to hurt yourself or someone else. You don't want that, do you, Mary?"

She was staring at the floor, feet kicking nervously like a small child.

"But I have to drive. How am I going to get where I have to be? I have to drive!"

"Don't worry, Mother," I said, trying to reassure her. "We'll find people to take you wherever you want to go."

Her dark eyes glaring at me, she snapped. "This is your doing isn't it?"

"No, Mary," her doctor said, quietly trying to calm her while at the same time taking the focus off me, "I ordered the driving test, remember? Now, Mary, this means you can't drive anymore."

"You mean at all?" she asked frantically, trying desperately to salvage something from the situation.

"No, Mary, not at all. It isn't safe for you to drive."

The fifteen-mile ride home seemed interminable, made even longer by the icy silence of my mother. Finally at her house I said, "OK, Mother, you're going to have to give me your car keys."

"I'm not giving you my keys," she snapped.

"But the doctor said you can't drive. You have to give me your keys."

"I'm not giving you my keys."

"Are you going to drive?"

"Yes."

"The doctor said you can't drive, and I'm not leaving here without your keys."

"Then you better take off your coat, because I'm not giving you my keys."

I knew that I had pushed her too far. I almost always did,

because it was part of the game. Her hackles were up, and nothing I said now would make any difference. It would be up to Peggy to get her to cooperate. This was the point when, as a teenager, the fighting with my mother would have turned physical and my father would have stepped in to separate us. Mother was nearly eighty and the thought of kicking, biting, and pulling hair seemed excessive. Besides, I wasn't entirely convinced she couldn't take me in a fight now.

"Fine," I said and stomped out. She thought it was over, but she didn't know I had her spare car keys. Dan brought me back to Mother's house, where I slipped into her garage and drove her car away without being detected. Once safely at home, I pulled her car inside my garage, closed the electric door, and parked my car in the driveway behind it. Her car was not going anywhere until Peggy came the next day. My human ego liked that I had one-upped her.

"That was easier than I expected," I told Dan. "I thought we would have a scene with this little old lady chasing me down the street screaming obscenities at me."

"Yeah, that went pretty smoothly. But I wonder if it might not be a good idea to call the police department and explain what happened just to be safe."

Dan is not normally an alarmist, so I made the call.

I didn't hear anything from my mother. I expected her to at least call and scream at me. I was prepared for a fight, but I found the silence to be eerie.

I called Peggy. "Mother wouldn't agree to stop driving, so I took her car and locked it in my garage. We can decide what to do when you get here tomorrow."

"That's fine. I'll call you when I get there."

Peggy called Friday when she arrived at my mother's. "Man, is she ever mad!"

"Should I come over?" I asked.

"No. She's way too mad. Let me try to calm her down. Maybe we can have lunch tomorrow."

"OK. Call me and let me know what's happening."

When I didn't hear from Peggy on Saturday morning, I called. "How are things going?"

"Tense." She was speaking barely above a whisper.

"Are we going to lunch? Should I come over?"

"No. She's too angry. I'll call you later."

I didn't hear from Peggy again until she showed up at my house on Sunday afternoon.

"It's been awful. She's really, really angry. She had Jim take her to the police station and actually tried to have you arrested for stealing her car, but you had already called them so they wouldn't do anything. That made her even angrier. And she's really mad because you referred to her as an elderly woman in the newspaper ad. She was mad about the whole ad. She was mad about the agreement you made me sign. She was mad about everything."

"Well, she's almost eighty. She is an elderly woman. How else would you describe her? Did you tell her that we agreed I should place the ad? Did you tell her you read it first and approved it before I ran it?"

"Well, no."

"Did you tell her you knew I was taking the car and agreed with that too?"

"Well, no."

"So you let me take the entire blame for the whole thing?!" I screamed.

"You don't understand. It isn't easy."

"No! You don't understand. All you would have had to do was say that we agreed to this. It would have diffused the whole situation, but instead you left me holding the bag. You just sat there and didn't say anything. You let her believe this was all my doing and that you didn't have anything to do with it. The only reason I'm doing any of this in the first place is because I'm in town. She doesn't even like me. You're just as responsible as I am, but you let me take the blame for all of it."

"Well, I'm not strong like you," she sobbed.

"Well, you're going to have to be because I'm through. You've done this to me for the last time. From now on, her care is your responsibility. I'm not going to be involved in any way. I won't be taking her to any more doctors' appointments; I won't be lining up helpers; I won't be handling it when people call with the crazy things she's done. In fact, I don't even want to be a part of this family. She never liked me to begin with; you were always Perfect Peggy. Our whole lives you let me take the blame for everything. I'm not doing it anymore. I've finally learned that lesson. You're going to continue setting me up and letting me take the blame for as long as I allow you to. Well, I'm not playing the game anymore. Any calls I get regarding Mother, I'm referring to you. I'm not going to be involved in her care ever again. She's all yours."

I can't remember ever being that angry. Peggy was just playing the game the way we always did in the past. I thought I changed the rules, but I obviously forgot to tell Peggy.

"Why are you being so mean to me?" she sobbed.

"I'm not being mean to you. You've brought this on yourself by always using me as a shield to hide behind to protect yourself. I'm not doing it anymore. It's time for you to take responsibility for your own actions."

Peggy left, and Dan and I returned the car to my mother's garage, the extra keys inside. I wrote Mother's attorney and informed him that I was no longer willing to serve as her power of attorney. When she killed someone with her car, I didn't want to be the person they called with the news.

On the surface it would appear that I finally grasped the concept of our sacred contract and took the necessary steps to end it. That's only partially true because I played my role in such a way that I still got to be the victim, perhaps even a martyr, a notch or two up on the evolutionary scale. I refused to be sucked into any more of the dramas with Mother and Peggy, but instead of refusing to accept blame and letting it go, I basked in self-righteous victim energy.

I didn't talk to my mother for about three months. I wasn't angry with her, because she responded in exactly the way I expected. Dan and I thought it was funny, even clever, that she tried to have me arrested for stealing her car. We laughed at the prospect of the police showing up at my door, weapons drawn, hauling me away in hand-cuffs and leg irons, charged with grand theft auto. I didn't contact Mother because having any semblance of a normal relationship with her would have diminished my role as martyr.

I understood what giving up her car meant to Mother, and I knew she wasn't capable of understanding that I had been trying to help her. She probably wouldn't have understood before the stroke, and after there was no chance. What I didn't understand was that I manipulated the drama in a manner in which it was certain to fail.

People continued to call me for a while to report my mother's bizarre behavior or to tell me she was still driving. As she had more small strokes, her behavior became even more erratic. Several merchants called to say she had tried to pay bills with cancelled checks. Two banks called to tell me she had demanded money from accounts she didn't have. In one instance, she had never had an account with the bank; in the other, she had closed the account previously. I smugly gave the callers Peggy's number. I don't know if they called her, but eventually they stopped calling me.

Finally in May, my mother sent me a Mother's Day card. Most people would consider that to be odd, but my mother was never conventional. At the bottom of the card she wrote, "I miss you. I'm sorry about our misunderstanding."

I wrote back and told her that I didn't classify trying to have me arrested for grand theft auto as a "misunderstanding," but I accepted her apology. Even though it truly didn't bother me, I kept the car issue alive so that I could continue to be a martyr. I told her I would never be involved in any aspect of her care again, but if she would like to try being friends, going to lunch or movies or shopping, the things mothers and daughters normally do, I would be willing to try. It was an unusual offer. In my entire life my mother and I had never done any of those things together, but on the other hand, I don't suppose most other mothers and daughters had the pleasure of hand-to-hand combat like we did.

Although I didn't see her often, our relationship became friendly and comfortable as I stepped further out of that victim energy. I called her at least once a week, and occasionally she called me, usually at the last possible minute, to invite me to accompany her to the symphony or a play to which she had tickets. It was obvious that she had already called everyone else she could think of and turned to me as a last resort. I didn't mind. Occasionally she would call me to pick her up from the body shop where her car was being repaired because of something she had hit. Fortunately, it was never a person. Our relationship was never what most mothers and daughters would consider normal, but with the sacred contract we chose, it was enough.

35
When You
See the Light

When Mother's older sister, Helen, passed over, the minister asked if I would jot down some notes about Helen to read at her memorial service. I agreed to say a few words, but warned him that they would be whatever spirit moved me to say at the time rather than something I had prepared. He looked concerned, knowing that my spiritual views don't necessarily follow traditional church doctrine. With either a leap of faith or lapse in judgment, he nonetheless called on me to speak.

As I stood before the small group gathered in the church, I realized that most of them had never known Helen. At almost ninety-two, Helen's contemporaries had already gone home. The people at the service were there to offer support to her daughters, Patty and Carla, and to my mother. I knew that any message spirit gave me would be directed toward the family, but I still didn't know what that might be.

As I began to speak, I told about the last time Carla and I had been together at my mother's eightieth birthday party. At the time I commented to Carla that her mother was surprisingly alert for ninety. Carla responded in typical daughterly exasperation.

"Yes, but she tells the same stories over and over and over again. I can hardly stand to hear them anymore."

As I continued speaking, I acknowledged to Carla and Patty that Helen also told me the same stories over and over again, but that I was certain they were not the same stories she told them.

Because they were her daughters, Helen would voice the frustrations and discomfort of trying to function in her aging body. She would complain that she missed her house and friends in Wapakoneta and wished she had never agreed to move to the assisted-living facility near Patty's where she spent the last year of this life. She seemed to forget that all of her friends were gone and that she had moved because she could no longer care for herself.

"No. The stories she told me over and over," I said, "were about how much she loved you both and how proud she was of you. She told me how much she appreciated the way you took care of her and that she was thankful for all you did. And I knew it was her truth because she told me these things every time I saw her."

I talked about the irony of how we complain to the people we love and only tell other people, sometimes near strangers, how we really feel about our loved ones. Instead, I said, we should be telling our true feelings to the people we love while they are still here to appreciate them.

It was at that moment I heard the voice softly speak the unfamiliar words: "Mother, I love you." I was so taken aback that my initial impulse was to look around for the kind stranger who had obviously entered the room undetected. I quickly realized, of course, that the voice as well as the words were mine. More importantly, I realized that the more than fifty years of hurt and anger between us no longer mattered. They were part of our sacred contract. And I knew that as I spoke those words, they were true.

Mother and I both seemed to realize that we would never completely resolve our differences in what remained of this lifetime. The divisions were too deep and the time too short to completely heal our relationship and resolve our sacred contract. Even though they were not without a few bumps, I cherished our last few months together.

Mother chose to experience a massive stroke that left her paralyzed, unable to speak or even swallow. She and I never had many in-depth conversations, but I had no doubt what she would want in this situation. Whenever she would visit a friend in a nursing home who had chosen a similar fate, Mother would make it a point to stop at my house. Visibly shaken, she would tell me, "I don't ever want to end up like that. Promise me you won't ever let anyone see me looking like that with that droopy face. That's awful. I would hate that."

Mother was a vain, almost narcissistic woman. How interesting that she chose the precise situation she feared most, helpless and pathetic from the human perspective. I knew what she told me, but since the famous "grand theft auto" incident, I no longer had her power of attorney. The final irony of Mother's life was going to be that the decision on her fate was now solely in Peggy's hands. In her sacred contract, Peggy agreed to play the role of victim by avoiding making decisions. Mother was giving her an enormous and dramatic opportunity to complete her contract. It was a beautiful act of love.

I was apprehensive about what Peggy would do, but I set my fear aside knowing that whatever her decision, nothing could happen that we all had not agreed to prior to this earthwalk. I didn't know if she had ever had the "don't let anyone see me like that" conversation with Mother, or if she would have the strength to honor it even if she had. Nonetheless, the decision about Mother's care would be Peggy's alone, and it would not be an easy one.

Peggy arrived at the hospital with a copy of the Living Will Mother signed nearly fifteen years before when my father was still in the body. In the intervening years, Mother had remarried and divorced. The name on the old document was still Peterson, and the hospital would not accept it. Peggy would have to make the decision herself. She was faced with several options, none of them pleasant from the human perspective. Because the stroke was massive and, according to the doctors, irreversible, Mother could not swallow. In the short term, the hospital could insert a feeding tube in her throat and provide fluids intravenously to keep her body alive. The long-term solution would be to surgically insert a feeding tube into her stomach. The quality of her life would be questionable, but she could live for years until the next stroke or other major complication took her life. The other choice, the "final solution" as it were, was to remove fluids and medication and allow nature to take its course. Mother would slowly starve to death, although the doctors assured us she would not be in pain. Her ex-husband, Jim, wanted to keep her alive no matter what her condition. He asked that Peggy have the feeding tube inserted and volunteered to take Mother to his home and care for her as he had done with his first wife when she became ill. His offer was genuine. He would have done his best to care for her and it provided Peggy with a viable alternative to allowing Mother to pass over.

Mother was awake at least part of the time, waving her good arm around and making low guttural sounds that were totally unintelligible. She was trying to communicate, but it was impossible to understand what she was trying to tell us.

Peggy and I discussed the options, and without pressuring her, I told her what I believed Mother would want. Still, the decision was Peggy's. Without hesitation Peggy refused to allow the feeding tube or any other extraordinary means of prolonging Mother's earthwalk. She would honor Mother's wishes and allow her to pass over with as much dignity as possible. It was a threshold moment for Peggy.

We transferred Mother to the same nursing home where Dan's mother spent her final days and we called in hospice care which provided oxygen, Ativan to calm her, and liquid morphine to make her more comfortable.

For more than two weeks we kept a bedside vigil with Mother. Unlike my father's final days when I sat alone at the hospital, Peggy was there much of the time, alternating every few days between the nursing home and her job in Lancaster. This time, of course, we knew what the outcome would be. We knew Mother was going to pass over; the only question was how quickly.

Peggy and I shopped together for Mother's burial dress, a festive one with sparkles that looked as if she were about to step onto the dance floor. We planned the funeral and chose the flowers—an arrangement of dozens of roses in every color imaginable. Mother loved roses. She had a beautiful garden that she had tended with love and pride. It was a healing time for Peggy and me, a time when we renewed our childhood bond.

When we were alone, I sat by Mother's bed and talked with her. I told her that I loved her and forgave her. Of course, because we agreed to all of our experiences together, there was nothing to forgive. I said it to comfort her human ego and make her passing easier. I also sang gentle nurturing songs to her from "Songs for the Inner Child" by Shaina Noll or her favorite hymns from a hymnal I found at the nursing home. In the end Mother did not allow any of us to be with her when she transitioned from this earthwalk. When

I left her bedside for the last time, just hours before she passed over,
I kissed her and said:

"I love you, Mother. Thank you for participating in my dramas.
You played your part well, and I honor you for that. When you see
the light, run toward it as fast as you can."

I'm certain she did.

36
Choices

The years since Mother passed over have been ones of great progress for both Peggy and me. We have made steps that I don't believe either of us could have made at this particular juncture without her passing. For me, there was always too much human anger and mistrust between Mother and me to heal during this earthwalk, no matter what our contract. We went as far as we could together encumbered by our human egos and emotions.

It would have been difficult to publish this book while mother was still in the body because her human ego would have felt embarrassment and, at that time, mine might have enjoyed that. Before her passing we had many heated discussions about it, but now she is not only supportive, but helpful.

For Peggy, Mother has become somewhat like Ian with the hot-poker-up-the-butt approach, always poking and prodding her to move forward, out of her comfort zone. Peggy has left her husband of thirty-six years and moved to Wapakoneta. She is beginning a new life on her own, filled with possibilities. Mother takes credit for setting the situation in motion that convinced Peggy to make the move.

Even after all these years on the other side, my father is still living in fear and darkness, which is, of course, his choice. As Ruth Renkel said, "Never fear shadows. They simply mean there's a light shining somewhere nearby." It is fine for him, but it no longer works for me. He is the equivalent of a crazymaker in spirit form for me, and our energy is no longer compatible. I love him and honor him for agreeing to participate in my drama this lifetime, but I don't want him around me or my loved ones because he encourages human turmoil.

As for Mother, she is doing well on the other side. For as unhappy and dysfunctional as she was during her last earthwalk, she embraced the light quickly upon her return, although not without some snags. After her passing she kept appearing in readings with a variety of different mediums, apologizing for how badly she treated me.

"I'm so sorry! I'm so sorry!" she would say. "I didn't understand."

I understood our contract together, and I would have thought being out of the human body, Mother would have also. I knew that she had agreed to provide a non-nurturing, emotionally and verbally abusive environment to give me the opportunity to discover self-love. I couldn't imagine a less-nurturing individual than my mother was to me in this lifetime. I didn't comprehend why she would feel the need to apologize. Mother unquestionably fulfilled her commitment to me. The difficulty she was facing was that she carried her role beyond the scope of what I needed to learn my lessons. I could have learned non-nurturing with far less abuse than she provided. She was not intentionally cruel, but overzealous. Apparently jealousy is a lesson her soul has been working on for many lifetimes, and has not yet mastered. Confronted by so formidable a rival for my father's affection, Mother overreacted to the situation, and was far more abusive to me than necessary to fulfill our agreement. The consequence is that she is in a sort of intensive study program to work on her jealously issues and learn how to deal with them better during her next earthwalk. It is also likely that she will have to return in the "victim" role of a similar abuse scenario in her next life.

According to Dr. Michael Newton, in his book *Destiny of Souls*, a guiding principle in the spirit world is that wrongdoing, whether intentional or unintentional on the part of all souls, will need to be addressed in some form in a future life. He writes:

"This is not considered punishment or even penance as much as an opportunity for karmic growth. There is no hell for souls, except perhaps on Earth."

It would appear I chose a difficult human experience for this earthwalk, and perhaps I did. To me, it seems more likely that the more difficult the lessons tackled, the greater the opportunity for growth. I choose to view my experiences as adventures on an unusually exciting journey. The point is, of course, that the journey is about choice and how we view the choices we make.

I am reminded of a weight-conscious friend I used to have lunch with on a regular basis. The woman is not tiny, but I probably outweigh her by at least fifty pounds. Every lunch was the same. We would order approximately the same thing, always including a rich dessert. With every bite she would belittle herself. "I'm such a hog! I have no business eating this! Do you realize how many calories are in this? Probably a million in every bite! No wonder I'm so damn fat!" Yet she continued to eat. I on the other hand sat quietly, savoring every bite of my magnificent dessert. In the end, we consumed the same amount of fat and calories, but we had entirely different experiences.

While the Universe might provide the specific dramas for each of our lessons, and continue providing them in increasing degrees of intensity until we learn the lesson, we always have a choice. We can choose to believe horrible things are done to us, trapping us in victim mode, or we can acknowledge that the experiences are always provided for us so that we can learn the lessons we came to learn. We can respond with love or fear with the full knowledge that our choice will mold our experience into the lessons we learn.

Each of our journeys is a solo trip intertwined with the loving souls who have agreed to participate in our dramas on Classroom Earth. I have chosen a wide variety of methods to help my soul advance, to aid in awakening from both my birth- and trauma-induced amnesias.

Writing has far and away proven to be the most powerful tool for me in shedding the victim energy and stepping into my spiritual power. In the three years it took me to complete this book I believed I was finished three other times. Just as I would be about to publish, the Universe would jump in with a human distraction such as my mother's passing or some other family situation because it knew neither I nor the book was ready to face the public. My own forward progress is most evident in reading the earlier drafts, which were dark and angry litanies of every event in my life I considered humiliating, detailing the horrible things that had been done "to me." The band director practically raped me in the band room. I was terrified and later ostracized by the community. Terrible Tim was truly terrible. The man with whom I became involved when we moved from California was old and vile to the point that the relationship appeared incestuous. In fact, he was handsome and charismatic, and our contract involved us coming together when in our human experiences we were both lonely and vulnerable, both in marriages that we needed to either repair or release. There were previously several chapters dealing with nothing but incest and recounting detail after detail of the "abuse." All of the stories were true as I knew them at the time, but with each new draft I stepped further out of the victim energy and closer to the light. The negativity was no longer a part of who I discovered I am.

Perhaps the most significant change is that all of the earlier drafts began with the flashbacks and abuse. The fact that neither appear until well into the second half of this book is indicative of how little importance they now have in my life. This is no longer a book about abuse or even healing, but rather about making the choice to step out of fear. Writing has been an integral part of letting that happen in my own earthwalk.

Although I have tried a variety of modalities that are both traditional and non-traditional, none of them have been either easy or fast. That second step forward has saved me many times from the effects of that one step back. Escaping the illusion has taken years of intense work, although the struggle became easier when I finally learned to stop struggling. Some of the things I tried were extremely helpful, and others simply didn't resonate with me. I have only included the ones here that I have personally found to be helpful. They might or might not work for anyone else. We each have the opportunity to choose from the myriad of options available and proceed with what works for us. There are no right or wrong choices, only different outcomes, each of which will add to our education on this beautiful Classroom Earth. We can savor the dessert or hate ourselves for eating it.

Perhaps the most important lesson I have learned is that only love is real and anything else is just an illusion created to provide more learning opportunities. While this has certainly not always been the case, when I am faced with multiple choices I try hard to pick the one that comes from love. When I do, I am never disappointed with the outcome. And I remind myself daily that, as with everything on Classroom Earth, happiness is a choice.

Peace.

Recommended Reading

Bodine, Echo. *Echoes of the Soul*. Novato: New World Library, 1999.

Cameron, Julia. *The Artist's Way: A Spiritual Path to Higher Creativity*. New York: Penguin Group, 1995.

Hay, Louise. *You Can Heal Your Life*. Santa Monica: Hay House, 1985.

Magi, Aria. *The Lulilities and the Star of Seven Rays*. Sedona: Lulilite Productions, 2005. (Children's Book.)

Myss, Caroline. *Sacred Contracts: Awakening Your Divine Potential*. New York: Harmony House, 2001.

Nemeth, Maria, Ph.D., *The Energy of Money*. New York: Ballantine Wellspring, 1999.

Newton, Michael, Ph.D., *Journey of Souls*. St. Paul: Llewellyn Wordwide, 1994. Or any other book by Dr. Newton.

Ruiz, Don Miguel. *The Four Agreements*. San Rafael: Amber-Allen Publishing, 1997.

Saloff, Jamie, *Transformational Healing: Five Surprisingly Simple Keys*

Designed to Redirect Your Life Toward Wellness, Purpose, and Prosperity, Sent Books, Saloff Enterprises, Edinboro, PA, 2005.

Sohn, David Wm., *Escaping the Labyrinth.* LIFETOOLS Publishers, 2004.

Tolle, Eckhart. *The Power of Now.* Novato: New World Library, 1999.

Van Praagh, James. *Talking to Heaven.* New York: Dutton, A member of The Penguin Group, 1997. Or any other book by Mr. Van Praagh.

Virtue, Doreen, Ph.D., *Healing With the Angels.* Santa Monica: Hay House, 1999. Or any other book by Dr. Virtue.

Wallach, George C., *Harvest of Illusion.* Phoenix: HighSight Publishing, 2003.

Zukav, Gary. *The Seat of the Soul.* New York: Fireside, Simon and Shuster, 1989.

Printed in the United States
40307LVS00006B/130-513